PRAYER IS THE KEY

DR. VICTOR MEBELE

WestBow®
PRESS
A DIVISION OF THOMAS NELSON
& ZONDERVAN

Unless otherwise noted, all scripture is from the 21st Century King James Version of the Bible.

WestBow Press books may be ordered through booksellers or by contacting:

WestBow Press
A Division of Thomas Nelson & Zondervan
1663 Liberty Drive
Bloomington, IN 47403
www.westbowpress.com
1 (866) 928-1240

ISBN: 978-1-4908-8201-7 (sc)
ISBN: 978-1-4908-8202-4 (hc)
ISBN: 978-1-4908-8200-0 (e)

Library of Congress Control Number: 2015908339

Print information available on the last page.

WestBow Press rev. date: 6/9/2015

CONTENTS

ACKNOWLEDGEMENT

I give all the glory to God for this piece of work that He has released through me. Without Him, it would not have been possible. His grace has made this possible. All my inspiration in writing comes from God, and all honors I give to Him.

PREFACE

Prayer Is the Key is a dynamic book full of powerful insights and real-life testimonials, which show the extraordinary life that is available to us through prayer.

Author Dr. Victor Mebele, originally from Nigeria but now somewhat of a globetrotter, preaches his sermons of prayer to anyone who will listen. In his book, he emphasizes the importance of doing life God's way. Throughout the Bible, God gives instructions on prayer, fasting and living a life that is truly dynamic. Dr. Mebele reiterates these truths by providing scripture references and testimonies of lives that were set free from discontent, financial struggles and danger by following God's instructions and living the kind of life He has told us to live.

Have you been praying the same prayer for years with no answer from God? It is time you picked up *Prayer Is the Key* and read its pages to find out how to move past a life full of unanswered prayers and move into a life that is exciting, dynamic and full of possibility.

DEDICATION

This book is dedicated to Dr. Morris Cerullo, who taught me what prayer really is.

INTRODUCTION

Many prayers are going on daily in churches, mosques, schools and other public places, but few answers are recorded. This was my quest after my conversion as a Christian in the year 1995. This led to my enlistment in Morris Cerullo Prayer Strike Force in The Netherlands where I learned the acts of prayer from the apostle of prayer in our generation: Dr. Morris Cerullo.

Prayer is one of the greatest tools God has placed in the hands of men to control Heaven and Earth, and it is very unfortunate that many believers does not know this truth. No wonder we have few gatherings in our churches when we call for prayer meetings. True prayer is what I call "the telephone line of God" if properly offered.

We all know that everything God does is based on principles, and prayer is not excluded. The result of a true prayer is an answer from Heaven, which is a confirmation that God heard you when you prayed. Now the question is why do so many prayers in our time remain unanswered? Does it mean that God has preferences? What are the reasons behind answered and unanswered prayers? Is prayer really important to the life of a believer?

In PRAYER IS THE KEY, you will discover the answers to the above questions. Many have written about prayer but have no proof of one answered prayer in their lives. PRAYER IS THE KEY is a proof producer book with testimonies of answered prayers in each chapter, both in the life of the author and others who were taught what consistent effectual prayer is. Jesus demonstrated prayer, and when His disciples saw His prayers answered like never before in the history of man, they cried out "Lord teach us to pray."

Dr. Victor Mebele is an apostle of prayer who has demonstrated that God answers prayer in his life (testimonies included in this book). Others who sat under his teaching on prayer are demonstrating the same thing; whose testimonies are also recorded in this book with pictures to prove them. PRAYER IS THE KEY takes you away from traditional or religious prayer theory books to the altar of prayer and reveals to you what you must do and how to do it in order to get the desired result. As a believer, there is nothing you can do that will effect humanity until your prayer lifestyle is structured and backed up with discipline just like Jesus while He walked on Earth in Israel.

And in the morning, rising up a great while before day,
He went out and departed into a solitary place, and
there prayed. —Mark 1:35

I know that your life will never be the same at the end of reading this book if you adhere to what you discover. Shalom.

CHAPTER ONE

The Importance Of Prayer In a Christian's Life

Prayer is very important in a Christian's life; in this chapter I will be discussing some of them. But first, let us keep in mind that prayer is a command and not an option for any Christian who wants to live successfully.

> *Then He taught, saying to them, "Is it not written, 'My house shall be called a house of prayer for all nations'? But you have made it a 'den of thieves.* —Mark 11:17

> *Then He spoke a parable to them that men always ought to pray and not lose heart.* —Luke 18:1

The following show the importance of prayer in a Christian's life:

I. **Prayer brings divine direction**: Since God is all knowing, He knows the beginning till the end of every destiny as stated in Isaiah 46: 9-10:

> *Remember the former things of old, For I am God, and there is no other; I am God, and there is none like Me, Declaring the end from the beginning, And*

> *from ancient times things that are not yet done, Saying,*
> *'My counsel shall stand, And I will do all My pleasure.*

Through prayer He brings divine directions to us in order for us to walk successfully in all He has purposed for us. Secondly, prayer helps us to avoid unnecessary delay in life. You can agree with me that if two people are travelling on an unknown road and one has a road map and the other does not, the one with the road map will arrive at their destination before the other. God has the road map of our destiny and this road map is often revealed only to those who communicate with God. We can see that the men and women who depended on God's road map in the Bible were successful.

> *You will show me the path of life: In Your presence*
> *is fullness of joy; at your right hand are pleasures*
> *forevermore.* —Psalm 16:11

> *The Lord is my shepherd; I shall not want.* —Psalm 23:1

It is very clear in the above scriptures that when God directs your life, victory is sure. King David was a man who never lost any battle and was never in need because God was his shepherd. There is a way that seems right to every man, but man is very much limited in the outcome of "his tomorrow" because he is man. Only God knows the beginning till the end; therefore, it is very wise to commit our journey on Earth into His hands in order to arrive successfully.

> *There is a way that seems right to a man, but its end*
> *is the way of death.* —Proverbs 14:12.

> *Thus says the Lord, your Redeemer, the Holy One of*
> *Israel: I am the Lord your God who teaches you to profit,*
> *who leads you by the way you should go.* —Isaiah 48:17

Divine direction has so many advantages and they are as follows:

A. **Success**. Success is inevitable when God directs you. God is the only one that knows the end from the beginning; therefore, when He directs you, be sure that you are coming out successfully, no matter how it may look physically (Isaiah 46:9-10).

> *This Book of the Law shall not depart from your mouth, but you shall meditate in it day and night, that you may observe to do according to all that is written in it. For then you will make your way prosperous, and then you will have good success.* —Joshua 1:8

B. **Unusual blessing**. When God directs you, He leads you to the blessings He has hidden for you even before the foundation of the Earth. Secondly, the blessings of the Lord enumerated in Deuteronomy 28:1-14 are only for those who yield to the voice of the Lord. Yielding to His voice is simply allowing Him to direct your life.

> *But as it is written, eye has not seen, nor ear heard, nor have entered into the heart of man the things which God has prepared for those who love Him.*
>
> *But God has revealed them to us through His Spirit. For the Spirit searches all things, yes, the deep things of God.* —1 Corinthians 2:9-10

C. **Protection**. When God directs you, He positions His angels to protect you.

> *The angel of the LORD encamps all around those who fear Him and delivers them.* —Psalm 34:7

> *Behold, I send an angel before you to keep you in the way and to bring you into the place which I have prepared.* —Exodus 23:20

D. Preservation and supernatural performance with peace. The world we live in today is full of struggles and stress because of human demands. Many people out of stress have taken their lives prematurely while many are in hospitals because of depression that came as a result of human struggles. God promised peace and strength to His children as they go about His business on planet Earth.

> *Peace I leave with you, my peace I give to you; not as the world gives do I give to you. Let not your heart be troubled, neither let it be afraid.* —John 14:27

God wants to direct us in every aspect of our lives, but we must be ready to meet the requirements before He will lead. Some of the requirements are as follows:

1. **You must be willing to be a sheep.** One of the characters of sheep is that they are totally dependent on the shepherd. Until you become a sheep, the Lord will not lead you. He is not going to follow your own way; it is too low for Him. You have to be a sheep and the shepherd will guide you into the green grass.

> *The LORD is my shepherd; I shall not want. He makes me to lie down in green pastures: he leads me beside the still waters.* —Psalm 23:2

> *For as many as are led by the Spirit of God, these are sons of God.* —Romans 8:14

2. **You must embrace the ministry of the Holy Spirit.** He is the most effective guide on Earth today. He is God on Earth. He knows what you don't know, He sees what you don't see and He hears what you don't hear.

> *However, when He, the Spirit of truth, has come, He will guide you into all truth; for He will not speak on His own authority, but whatever He hears He will speak; and He will tell you things to come.* —John 16:13

3. **Embrace the Word.** To be guided properly you must embrace the integrity of God's Word. God means what He says and He says what He means. Every single instruction in His Word have been prepared to lead you in life, step by step until you succeed above your imagination: What must I do to be blessed? It is clear in the Word.

> *But he who looks into the perfect law of liberty and continues in it, and is not a forgetful hearer but a doer of the work, this one will be blessed in what he does.* —James 1:25

> *This Book of the Law shall not depart from your mouth, but you shall meditate in it day and night, that you may observe to do according to all that is written in it. For then you will make your way prosperous, and then you will have good success.* —Joshua 1:8.

4. **Be meek.** Meekness does not mean being quite or walking gently, Meekness means humility in your heart. Wrong or right, when God speak, you humble yourself and follow Him. God does speak to people who are proud in their heart. Example,

people who say 'this is what I have decided and I will not change it no matter who speaks to me. God's reply to such group is, "Carry on and we will see how far you will go."

> *Turn at my rebuke; surely I will pour out my spirit on you; I will make my words known to you. Because I have called and you refused, I have stretched out my hand and no one regarded, because you disdained all my counsel, and would have none of my rebuke, I also will laugh at your calamity; I will mock when your terror comes. When your terror comes like a storm, and your destruction comes like a whirlwind, when distress and anguish come upon you. Then they will call on me, but I will not answer; they will seek me diligently, but they will not find me.* —Proverbs 1:23-28

> *The humble He guides in justice, and the humble He teaches His way.* —Psalm 25:9

5. **Separate yourself often to seek Him in prayer.** God can only lead you when you relate with Him. You recognize the voice of your friends or family members because of close relationship; the same is true with God. He speaks to all of us but only those who relate with Him understand His voice (*Habakkuk 2:1-3, Jeremiah 29:11-13, 2 Samuel 5:18-19, 22-25*).
6. **Remain joyful.** When you remain joyful because of Christ in you, the peace of God will flood your heart, which opens your inner man to hear His voice (*Psalm 16:11, Psalm 22:3*).

II. **Another importance of prayer is that you can overcome temptation when you pray.** Prayer will help you overcome temptation. Jesus made this known to His disciples at the Garden of Gethsemane. We could see that when they ignored the warning of the Lord, and when the trial came, they all failed, but the only one who prayed (Jesus) overcame despite the magnitude of the temptation that the enemy threw on Him. Prayer-less Christians fall often into temptation. When you are too busy to pray, you will surely live a sinful life.

> *Watch and pray, lest you enter into temptation. The spirit indeed is willing, but the flesh is weak.* — Matthew 26:41

III. **Prayer destroys problems.** Not all prayers are effective on their targets. It takes the rightful key to open a door. Key equals knowledge in the Kingdom of God. In Hosea 4:6, God said, "My people perish for lack of knowledge." In Matthew 16:18-19, Jesus spoke about these keys to Peter after it was revealed to Peter that Jesus is the Son of God. When you have the understanding of the Word of God and know how to appropriate the promises of God in your prayers, success is inevitable. The word of God destroys the work of Satan (*1 John 15:14-15, Mark 9: 17-29*).

IV. **Prayer opens the Heavens; it opens the spiritual world to you.** The only weapon that penetrates through the galaxies of the universe and into the Heavens is prayer. It is a weapon given to man by God to control both Heaven and Earth, and until we make use of this weapon effectively, the will of God cannot be done on Earth. Prayer can do whatever God can do. Why? Prayers are simply returning the Word of God back to Him; and remember that the Bible says that God and His Word are the same (John 1:1). Prayer breaks every resistance of the enemy in the spiritual world to usher in the will of God on Earth. When we allow the Spirit of God to aid us in prayer, He reveals to us what Heaven has in the God's storehouse for us.

> *Likewise the Spirit also helpeth our infirmities; for we know not what we should pray for as we ought, but the*

Spirit itself maketh intercession for us with groanings which cannot be uttered. —Romans 8:26

But as it is written: "Eye hath not seen, nor ear heard, neither have entered into the heart of man the things which God hath prepared for them that love Him." But God hath revealed them unto us by His Spirit. For the Spirit searcheth all things, yea, the deep things of God. —1 Corinthians 2:9-10

And when the servant of the man of God had risen early and gone forth, behold, a host compassed the city both with horses and chariots. And his servant said unto him, "Alas, my master! What shall we do?" And he answered, "Fear not, for they that are with us are more than they that are with them." And Elisha prayed and said, "Lord, I pray thee, open his eyes, that he may see." And the Lord opened the eyes of the young man, and he saw; and behold, the mountain was full of horses and chariots of fire round about Elisha. —2 Kings 6:15-17

V. **Prayer will save you from the traps of your enemies.** Many Christians have died prematurely because of prayerlessness, but not because it is the will of God for them to be killed by the enemy. It is prayer that exposes your enemy. Listen to this testimony of mine.

In the year 2002, I was visiting my family in Nigeria, West Africa. As I was in prayer over this journey, the Lord revealed to me that I was going to be attacked and I might die. The Lord showed me two black scorpions that the enemy was going to use to kill me, and I killed one of the scorpions in this vision but the second scorpion escaped. So I was prepared in prayer over this issue. When I arrived to the village where my grandmother lived, many people gathered to welcome me in the evening, and because my grandmother had not seen me for eight years, she bought a goat and made soup for the people. As they were celebrating my home coming, I knew in my spirit that evil was imminent; I could perceive it. So I went to take my bath. The moment I stepped into the room I was going to sleep, I saw a huge black scorpion on top of my pillow. I said, "Yes, you are already exposed and now you have failed." I called for a knife and killed the scorpion. Then I went into prayer and slept till the following day. Early in the morning, a man walked up to me as I was about to enter my car. He said "Vic, I am sorry for yesterday's scorpion. I am a wizard but I found out yesterday that it is impossible to kill you." I looked at him eye to eye and said, "Don't ever try it again." He said, "Yes I will not," and walked away. Now imagine if I did not pray before embarking on this journey—I could have been killed like many evangelists who have lost their lives due to African witches and wizards. The power of divination and enchantments are still very strong in Africa, but these powers are not a match to the name of Jesus. They bow down to the name of Jesus when we pray. If we don't pray, when we confront them, they will kill us without mercy. And it is not because they are more powerful than God; it is just because we neglect to call down the power of God through prayer. Prayer saves us from every evil plan of Satan.

> *Then the king of Syria warred against Israel, and took counsel with his servants, saying, "In such and such a place shall be my camp." And the man of God sent unto the king of Israel, saying, "Beware that thou pass not such a place, for thither the Syrians are coming down." And the king of Israel sent to the place of which the man of God told him and warned him, and saved himself there, not once nor twice. Therefore the heart of the king of Syria was sore troubled by this thing; and he called his servants and said unto them, "Will ye*

not show me which of us is for the king of Israel?" And one of his servants said, "None, my lord, O king; but Elisha, the prophet who is in Israel, telleth the king of Israel the words that thou speakest in thy bedchamber.
—2 Kings 6:8-12

Prophet Elisha was a man of prayer, and as he prayed, God revealed and exposed the plans of Satan. In Luke 22, the plan of Satan against Peter was revealed to Jesus because He prayed. Peter could not see it and if not for the prayers of Jesus, the story of Peter could have ended at Jesus' crucifixion. We could not have read about the Peter who healed the blind man at the beautiful gate or Peter whose shadow healed the sick. But after this incident, Peter learned his lesson and embraced prayer after he was forgiven for denying the Lord. He became the apostle of prayer throughout the book of Acts.

And the Lord said, "Simon, Simon! Behold, Satan hath desired to have you, that he may sift you as wheat. But I have prayed for thee, that thy faith fail not; and when thou art converted, strengthen thy brethren." And Peter said unto Him, "Lord, I am ready to go with Thee, both into prison and to death." And He said, "I tell thee, Peter, the cock shall not crow this day before thou shalt thrice deny that thou knowest Me. —Luke 22:31-34

Now Peter and John went up together into the temple at the hour of prayer, being the ninth hour. And a certain man lame from his mother's womb was being carried, whom they laid daily at the gate of the temple, which is called Beautiful, to ask alms from those who entered into the temple. He, seeing Peter and John about to go into the temple, asked for alms. And Peter, fastening his eyes upon him with John, said, "Look on us." And he gave heed unto them, expecting to receive something from them.

Then Peter said, "Silver and gold have I none, but such as I have, I give thee: in the name of Jesus Christ of Nazareth, rise up and walk." And he took him by the right hand and lifted him up, and immediately his feet and ankle bones received strength. And leaping up, he stood and walked and entered with them into the temple, walking and leaping and praising God.
—Acts 3:1-8

Then the twelve called the multitude of the disciples unto them and said, "It is not fitting that we should leave the Word of God to serve tables. Therefore, brethren, look ye out among you for seven men of honest report, full of the Holy Ghost and wisdom, whom we may appoint over this business. But we will give ourselves continually to prayer and to the ministry of the Word. —Acts 6:2-4

Prayer is the key that exposes and stops the plans of the enemy against us.

VI. Prayer enforces prophecy. Many people in the church have wondered why thousands of prophesies over their lives failed to manifest. We should understand one thing: Satan does not know what is in the mind of God until it is spoken. In many places in the Bible, we find out that the moment a prophecy is released, the next action you will find out is Satan working through his agents to hinder what God has said.

When it was revealed to King Harold that Jesus was born, he went into action by killing all babies from 0-2 years in order to eliminate the Savior. Pharaoh tried to eliminate the Israelites when he discovered that they were becoming mightier than the Egyptians. The moment you are revealed to the enemy, he will fight you by all means to see that your destiny in God is aborted. But by prayer, we can enforce the prophecies over our lives and deal with every kingdom that may stand against the will of God. Paul reminded Timothy this in 1 Timothy 1:18. It takes warfare to get to the promise land. Those who refuse to fight die before the reach their promise land.

> *This charge I commit unto thee, son Timothy, according to the prophecies which went before concerning thee, that thou by them mightest wage a good warfare.* —1 Timothy 1:18

> *Rise ye up, take your journey and pass over the River Arnon. Behold, I have given into thine hand Sihon the Amorite, king of Heshbon, and his land. Begin to possess it, and contend with him in battle.* — Deuteronomy 2:24

> *And from the days of John the Baptist until now, the Kingdom of Heaven suffereth violence, and the violent take it by force.* —Matthew 11:12

VII. Prayer releases your rain, which signifies blessings. Until we pray, Heaven does not release rain. Prayer releases rain, which signifies blessing. Lack of prayer hinders our rain.

> *And Elijah said unto Ahab, "Get thee up, eat and drink; for there is a sound of abundance of rain." So Ahab went up to eat and to drink. And Elijah went up to the top of Carmel; and he cast himself down upon the earth and put his face between his knees,*

and said to his servant, "Go up now, look toward the sea." And he went up and looked, and said, "There is nothing." And he said, "Go again," seven times. And it came to pass at the seventh time, that he said, "Behold, there ariseth a little cloud out of the sea, like a man's hand." And he said, "Go up, say unto Ahab, 'Prepare thy chariot, and get thee down, that the rain stop thee not.'" And it came to pass in the meantime, that the heaven was black with clouds and wind, and there was a great rain. And Ahab rode, and went to Jezreel. —1 Kings 18:41-45*

Ask ye of the Lord rain in the time of the latter rain; so the Lord shall make bright clouds, and give them showers of rain, to everyone grass in the field. — Zechariah 10:1

He that ask shall receive.

VIII. **Prayer is one of the tools that establish the Kingdom of God.** A prayerful church is the only church that can fulfill the will of God on Earth. The only connection between Heaven and Earth is prayer and also it takes prayer to stop the adversary of the church.

In this manner therefore pray ye: Our Father who art in Heaven, hallowed be Thy name. Thy Kingdom come. Thy will be done on Earth, as it is in Heaven. —Matthew 6:9-10

But when they had commanded them to go outside the council, they conferred among themselves, saying, "What shall we do to these men? For indeed, that a notable miracle hath been done by them is manifest to all those who dwell in Jerusalem, and we cannot deny it. But so that it spread no further among the people, let us strictly threaten them, that they speak henceforth to no man in this name." And they called them back and commanded them not to speak at all nor teach in the name of Jesus. But Peter and John answered and said unto them, "Whether it be right in the sight of God to hearken unto you more than unto God, judge ye; for we cannot but speak the things which we have seen and heard."

So when they had further threatened them, they let them go, finding nothing for which they might punish them, because of the people; for all men glorified God for that which had been done. For the man was over forty years old on whom this miracle of healing was shown. And being let go, they went to their own company and reported all that the chief priests and elders had said unto them.

And when they heard this, they lifted up their voice to God with one accord and said, "Lord, Thou art God who hast made heaven and Earth and the sea and all that is in them, who by the mouth of Thy servant David hast said, 'Why did the heathen rage, and the people imagine vain things? The kings of the earth stood up, and the rulers were gathered together against the Lord and against His Christ.' For truly against Thy holy child Jesus, whom Thou hast anointed, both Herod and Pontius Pilate, with the Gentiles and the people of Israel, had gathered together to do whatsoever Thy hand and Thy counsel determined before to be done.

*And now, Lord, behold their threatenings, and grant
unto Thy servants that with all boldness they may speak
Thy Word, by stretching forth Thine hand to heal, and
that signs and wonders may be done by the name of
Thy holy child Jesus." And when they had prayed, the
place was shaken where they were assembled together;
and they were all filled with the Holy Ghost, and they
spoke the Word of God with boldness. —Acts 4:15-31*

IX. Holy Spirit Works only in Prayer Environment. When prayer
is neglected, the Holy Spirit leaves because He can only work in
the environment of prayer.

*These all continued with one accord in prayer and
supplication, with the women and Mary the mother of
Jesus, and with His brethren. —Acts 1:14*

*And when the day of Pentecost was fully come, they
were all with one accord in one place. And suddenly
there came a sound from heaven as of a rushing mighty
wind, and it filled all the house where they were
sitting. And there appeared unto them cloven tongues
as of fire, and it sat upon each of them. And they were
all filled with the Holy Ghost and began to speak in
other tongues, as the Spirit gave them utterance. —
Acts 2:1-4*

X. Prayer causes damage to the kingdom of darkness. When we
pray, the kingdom of darkness in our nations that are keeping
people away from the Kingdom of God will be destroyed. When
Heaven responds to the prayers of the saints, the kingdom of
darkness has no place to hide; it is total destruction.

Then the LORD put forth His hand and touched my mouth. And the LORD said unto me, "Behold, I have put My words in thy mouth. See, I have this day set thee over the nations and over the kingdoms to root out and to pull down, and to destroy and to throw down, to build and to plant. —Jeremiah 1:9-10

And when He had opened the seventh seal, there was silence in Heaven about the space of half an hour. And I saw the seven angels who stood before God, and to them were given seven trumpets. And another angel came and stood at the altar, having a golden censer; and there was given unto him much incense, that he should offer it with the prayers of all saints upon the golden altar, which was before the throne.

And the smoke of the incense, which came with the prayers of the saints, ascended up before God out of the angel's hand. And the angel took the censer, and filled it with fire from the altar, and cast it onto the earth; and there were voices and thunderings and lightnings, and an earthquake. —Revelation: 8:1-5

XI. You cannot grow as a Christian above your prayer level. Prayer is ordained by God as a means by which He does things through men on Earth. Prayer is God's weapon of accomplishing His plan for you.

"Prayer is the key to God's store houses of infinite grace and power." —R.A Torrey

CHAPTER TWO

The Principles of Answered Prayer, 1 John 5:14-15

There are lots of books written on the subject of prayer, and there are many people on Earth praying. Different religious groups pray three times a day and despite all the prayers that are going on, the world is still in the shape it is today. I use to believe that God hears all prayers until the Lord took me through the Bible to see the prayers that He answered and the principles that governed them. From that very day, answers to my prayers were no longer delayed. Many people pray but never have testimonies or evidence that God heard them. It makes them to wonder if God really hears prayers. Some have submitted to the saying that God's time is not our time, while others are religiously talking into the air and hoping that one day God will answer. Some have waited all their lifetime but never receive an answer from the Lord.

The Lord's desire is to answer our prayers, but our prayers must be based on His principles. Everything God does is based on principles as we know, and prayer is not excluded.

> *Now this is the confidence that we have in Him, that*
> *if we ask anything according to His will, He hears us.*
> *And if we know that He hears us, whatever we ask, we*

> *know that we have the petitions that we have asked of Him.* —1 John 5:14-15

The Principles of Answered Prayer

1. **The integrity of your heart**. You don't judge your heart by what you think that is right or by what you feel. You judge your heart by the Word of God. When you keep your heart according to what the Word says and pray, God will definitely hear and answer. In Psalm 24:3-5, the Word stated clearly that only those with a clean heart are permitted into the presence of God. Many people have different ways of perceiving or seeing issues on Earth; therefore, what I may consider right might not be agreed with by another person who has a different opinion about it. So how do we measure a clean heart since every individual has his or her own way of judging wrong or right in our various hearts? God has a standard of a clean heart in His Word, and no matter what we think or believe, until our hearts are transformed into the Word standard, it will not be accepted by God. In Psalm 66:18, David stated by the Holy Ghost that when iniquity is found in our hearts, God will not answer our prayers.

    > *If I regard iniquity in my heart, the Lord will not hear.* —Psalm 66:18

    Iniquity is sin. This means that if I harbor sin in my heart, my prayer will not be answered. There are lots of Christians disobeying the Word of God and never willing to repent. They spend hours in prayer, hoping to receive answers from God, but they never received. Why? Because sin separates us from God.

    > *Behold, the LORD's hand is not shortened, that it cannot save; nor His ear heavy, that it cannot hear.*

But your iniquities have separated you from your God;
and your sins have hidden His face from you, so that
He will not hear. —Isaiah 59:1-2

It is therefore necessary that we check our hearts before we go into prayer, and if we find anything that goes contrary with God's Word; we must repent of it and stay in meditation of the Word to deal with that issue before we pray. That is when our hearts are free and stay in the standard of a clean heart that is accepted before God.

How can a young man cleanse his way? By taking
heed according to your word. With my whole heart
I have sought you' Oh, let me not wander from your
commandments! Your word I have hidden in my heart
that I might not sin against you. —Psalm 119:9-11

Remember, O LORD, Your tender mercies and your
loving kindnesses, for they are from of old. Do not
remember the sins of my youth, nor my transgressions;
according to your mercy remember me, For Your
goodness' sake, O LORD. Good and upright is the LORD;
therefore He teaches sinners in the way. The humble
He guides in justice, and the humble He teaches His
way. All the paths of the LORD are mercy and truth,
to such as keep His covenant and His testimonies. For
Your name's sake, O LORD, pardon my iniquity, for
it is great.

Who is the man that fears the LORD? Him shall He
teach in the way He chooses. He himself shall dwell in
prosperity, and his descendants shall inherit the earth.
The secret of the LORD is with those who fear Him, and
He will show them His covenant. —Psalm 25:6-14

There is no sin that the Lord will not pardon, but it takes humility to accept that you are a sinner before Him and that you are willing to change. When He sees the humility of real repentance in your heart, He will pardon, hear your prayers and cause you to enjoy prosperity by manifestation of your request.

2. **When you keep the commandment**: In the Old Testament, the Ten Commandments of God are found in Exodus 20: 1-17. Commandments 1-5 deal with God, and commandments 6-10 deal with our neighbors. In the New Testament, in John 13:34-35, Jesus stated a new commandment: Love God and love your neighbor. If we go back to Exodus 20, the first 5 commandments that deal with God can be summarized to love just like Jesus said, because if you love God, you will not have another god beside Him, and you will not bow to a graven image except the only one true God and so on. The same applies to your neighbor; if you love your neighbor, you will not steal from him or take his wife or properties. This means that love is the basis of a successful Christian. Then in 1 John 3: 22-24, the issue of keeping the commandment came up if our prayers will be answered.

> *And whatever we ask we receive from Him, because we keep His commandments and do those things that are pleasing in His sight.* —1 John 3:22

For you to receive an answer to your prayer, you must walk in the love of God unconditionally. This is where many Christians fail in their prayer life. It is not an option, but a must. In the Old Testament, the death penalty is the judgment against those who break any of the Ten Commandments; the same applies in the New Testament, though Jesus paid the price of death for us. If you want to enjoy the blessings of the price He paid, you must keep the commandment of love. Without that, there is no manifestation, no proof to show that you are in a covenant with the blood of Calvary. Christianity without unconditional love is religion and frustration. This is what we see today in the church—people are frustrated and they don't know why. The simple truth is that the only commandment that we are commanded to obey is broken every day. When you walk outside love, your prayer will not be answered.

> *And whatever we ask we receive from Him, because we keep His commandments and do those things that are pleasing in His sight.* —1 John 3:22

> *He who has my commandments and keeps them, it is he who loves me. And he who loves me will be loved by My Father, and I will love him and manifest myself to him.* —John 14:21

3. **Your knowledge of the Word.** Lack of knowledge or understanding of your new birth, your right standing with God, your right to use the name of Jesus, how to stand in the Word of God and steadfastness in confession has robbed many of their inheritance.

God answers prayers that are based on His covenant. When a Christian lacks knowledge of the Word of God, he will surely pray amiss just as James said.

> *My people are destroyed for lack of knowledge. Because you have rejected knowledge, I also will reject you from being priest for me; because you have forgotten the law of your God, I also will forget your children.* —Hosea 4:6

You ask and do not receive, because you ask amiss, that you may spend it on your pleasures. It is asking according to the will of God that guarantees answer and the will of God is simply the Word of God. When we know the Word, abide it and be a doer of it, answers to our prayers are guaranteed. *Now this is the confidence that we have in Him, that if we ask anything according to His will, He hears us. And if we know that He hears us, whatever we ask, we know that we have the petitions that we have asked of Him.* —1 John 5:14-15

> *If you abide in me, and my words abide in you, you will ask what you desire, and it shall be done for you. By this My Father is glorified, that you bear much fruit; so you will be my disciples.* —John 15:7-8.

Prayers are answered when we know who we are in Christ Jesus and when we use the right of the name of Jesus to get all that He paid for us. We are the righteousness of God in Christ Jesus, and we are commanded to come to the throne of grace and demand what Jesus paid for us in His name. Going to prayer with condemnation and fear will deny you your right in Christ Jesus. We are no longer slaves but sons and daughters of God through Christ Jesus. We belong to God, and God wants to glorify His name through us. Take away the "religious cap" and go with simplicity in boldness to the throne in the name of Jesus and demand what belongs to you.

> *Seeing then that we have a great High Priest who has passed through the heavens, Jesus the Son of God, let us hold fast our confession. For we do not have a High Priest who cannot sympathize with our weaknesses, but was in all points tempted as we are, yet without sin. Let us therefore come boldly to the throne of grace, that we may obtain mercy and find grace to help in time of need.* —Hebrews 4:14-16

> *Therefore remember that you, once Gentiles in the flesh, who are called uncircumcision by what is called*

the Circumcision made in the flesh by hands that at that time you were without Christ, being aliens from the commonwealth of Israel and strangers from the covenants of promise, having no hope and without God in the world. But now in Christ Jesus you who once were far off have been brought near by the blood of Christ. —Ephesians 2:11-13

Now, therefore, you are no longer strangers and foreigners, but fellow citizens with the saints and members of the household of God. —Ephesians 2:19

4. **Line up your confession with what you have prayed.** Words are powerful; they are seeds that bring either a good or bad harvest, depending on what you sow. One of the powerful principles of answered prayers is that men and women who prayed stayed in confession of what they prayed for or desired despite the circumstances that faced them.

Satan understands the power of words, so what he does is wait until we finish praying, and then he attacks us with circumstances contrary to what we prayed. The reason he does this is to cause us to abort our results through what we say. You can be praying that by the stripes of Jesus you were healed and the moment you stand up from the altar of prayer, the pain in your body will increase. You will likely yield to that pain and say things like, "This pain is killing me." You see your confession is not lining up with your prayer, and whatever you say, you will receive.

Death and life are in the power of the tongue, and those who love it will eat its fruit. —Proverbs 18:21

The sower sows the word. —Mark 4:14

> *Do not be deceived, God is not mocked; for whatever*
> *a man sows, that he will also reap.* —Galatians 6:7

For answers to come after prayer, we should resist every attempt by the enemy to cause us to use our mouth and destroy our answers. Rather, we should confess faith because we overcome him by our faith. Faith confession blows the fact away and establishes the truth. The pain is a fact, but the truth is that by His stripes you were healed of that pain.

> *So Jesus answered and said to them, "Have faith in*
> *God. For assuredly, I say to you, whoever says to this*
> *mountain, 'Be removed and be cast into the sea,' and*
> *does not doubt in his heart, but believes that those*
> *things he says will be done, he will have whatever he*
> *says. Therefore I say to you, whatever things you ask*
> *when you pray, believe that you receive them, and you*
> *will have them."* —Mark 11:22-24

> *For whatever is born of God overcomes the world. And*
> *this is the victory that has overcome the world—our*
> *faith.* —1 John 5:4

5. **Confess your sin.** When you sin, do not run away from God, but run to Jesus and confess the sin. He will cleanse you with His blood so that you can go to the throne of God in His righteousness as if nothing happened. It is a promise in 1 John 1:8-10.

> *If we say that we have no sin, we deceive ourselves,*
> *and the truth is not in us. If we confess our sins, He is*
> *faithful and just to forgive us our sins and to cleanse*
> *us from all unrighteousness. If we say that we have not*

sinned, we make Him a liar, and His word is not in us. —1 John 1:8-10

Unconfessed sin hinders answers to prayers. It separates us from God and causes Him to not hear us.

Behold, the Lord's *hand is not shortened, that it cannot save nor His ear heavy, that it cannot hear. But your iniquities have separated you from your God; and your sins have hidden His face from you, so that He will not hear.* —Isaiah 59:1-2

If I regard iniquity in my heart, the Lord will not hear. —Psalm 66:18

6. **Your Actions**. Faith is a fact and also an act. Faith that is not acted upon is like a body without the spirit. It will die and produce nothing. As we confess the promises, we should act on what we are confessing if we want to see manifestation. When the woman with the issue of blood heard about Jesus, she acted upon her confession. In the process of going, she met obstacles on the way, but she determined to keep acting until the manifestation took place. One, she was weak after losing blood for 12 years; two, on her way, she met the crowd that could have suggested to her to go home because there was no way she could penetrate the crowd with her stinking blood clothes; three, Jairus, the ruler of the synagogue was there; he could have ordered her to be stoned to death because it was a taboo in Israel for a person with such disease to be out in the public. All these obstacles were facing her but she kept her confession and action, and at the end, Jesus commended her faith.

Now a certain woman had a flow of blood for twelve years, and had suffered many things from many physicians. She had spent all that she had and was no better, but rather grew worse. When she heard about Jesus, she came behind Him in the crowd and touched His garment. For she said, "If only I may touch His clothes, I shall be made well."

Immediately the fountain of her blood was dried up, and she felt in her body that she was healed of the affliction. And Jesus, immediately knowing in Himself that power had gone out of Him, turned around in the crowd and said, "Who touched My clothes?"

But His disciples said to Him, "You see the multitude thronging you, and you say, 'Who touched Me?'"

And He looked around to see her who had done this thing. But the woman, fearing and trembling, knowing what had happened to her, came and fell down before Him and told Him the whole truth. And He said to her, "Daughter, your faith has made you well. Go in peace, and be healed of your affliction.
—Mark 5:25-34

7. **Forgiveness.** Learn to forgive others when they offend you. Offense does more harm to you than the person you are holding in your heart. When you refuse to forgive other people of whatever they did to you, God will not forgive you when you sin. Remember that no man is perfect; therefore, you will surely sin against God.

Now the Bible says that the wages of sin is death, which means when God refuses to forgive you, you will reap curses instead of blessing even when you cry to God in prayer to bless you. He will not alter His Word and send blessing when you have not obeyed

His command of forgiving others when you stand praying. He did not give any condition by which we must forgive, but He said if one offends you, you must forgive. Unforgiveness causes us to lose our blessing. If God has forgiven you and blessed and protected you, unforgiveness will remove His protection which opens the door for the enemy to take over and destroy us. Jesus spoke about this in Mark and in Matthew He revealed to us the cost of unforgiveness.

> *And whenever you stand praying, if you have anything against anyone, forgive him, then your Father in heaven may also forgive you your trespasses. But if you do not forgive, neither will your Father in heaven forgive your trespasses.* —Mark 11:25-26

> *But as he was not able to pay, his master commanded that he be sold, with his wife and children and all that he had, and that payment be made The servant therefore fell down before him, saying, 'Master, have patience with me, and I will pay you all.' Then the master of that servant was moved with compassion, released him, and forgave him the debt.*

> *But that servant went out and found one of his fellow servants who owed him a hundred denarii; and he laid hands on him and took him by the throat, saying, 'Pay me what you owe!' So his fellow servant fell down at his feet and begged him, saying, 'Have patience with me, and I will pay you all.' And he would not, but went and threw him into prison till he should pay the debt. So when his fellow servants saw what had been done, they were very grieved, and came and told their master all that had been done. Then his master, after he had called him, said to him, 'You wicked servant! I forgave you all that debt because you begged me. Should you*

> *not also have had compassion on your fellow servant,*
> *just as I had pity on you?' And his master was angry,*
> *and delivered him to the torturers until he should pay*
> *all that was due to him.*
>
> *"So My heavenly Father also will do to you if each of*
> *you, from his heart, does not forgive his brother his*
> *trespasses.* —Matthew 18:25-35.

Unforgiveness begins with offense and end with spiritual and physical death. It grows as follows:

Offense>>Resentment>>Unforgiving>>Root of bitterness>>Hate>> Spiritual death or dryness>>Physical death.

Many Christians pretend that they have forgiven but in reality, they have not. The following symptoms show that we have not forgiven those who offended us:

Thought of vengeance, we are happy when something bad happens to the person that hurts us, we constantly talk about the issue any time we are opportune, we express negative physical signs any time the name of the person is mention and we never see anything good from the person even when the person has done something good. Any time you see yourself exhibiting the above symptoms, know that you have not really forgiven; all you must do is to go to God in prayer to help you get over the hurt.

If you want to see your prayers answered quickly, do not play with unforgiveness. Be quick to forgive and pray for those who offend you. Ephesians 4:26 tells us to forgive people that offend us before the Sun goes down. The reason is so that the hurt does to progress to a stage of been rooted in our hearts because once we allow it to stay longer than 24 hours; it will progress and become more difficult to overcome.

8. **Strife.** Strife is the devil's master key for all troubles in hell to come upon a person. In James 3:16, the Bible says that strife opens door for every evil works. Unforgiveness leads to bitterness, which eventual gives birth to strife and strife gives birth to all evil works from hell. A person that walks in strife is always depressed and full of fear. Strife hinders your effectiveness in prayer and steals your faith that God is able to meet your needs according to His riches in glory. Strife causes disunity and prayer without agreement cannot be honored in Heaven.

> *Again I say to you that if two of you agree on Earth concerning anything that they ask, it will be done for them by My Father in heaven.* —Matthew 18:19

> *For where envy and self-seeking exist, confusion and every evil thing are there.* —James 3:16

> *Husbands, likewise, dwell with them with understanding, giving honor to the wife, as to the weaker vessel, and as being heirs together of the grace of life, that your prayers may not be hindered.* —1 Peter 3:7

Answers come quickly when husbands and wives forgive themselves and each other and pray in unity. The enemy understands this principle, and that is why he continues to create divisions in our homes and churches.

CHAPTER THREE

How to Enter God's Presence in Prayer

The same way kings and queens on Earth have protocols of entering into their presence, Our King of kings has also a protocol that allows you into His Presence during prayer. A lot of believers miss this protocol; and when it is omitted, every other thing concerning your prayers is nothing before God. The reason is because you miss the "pin code" of entering into His Presence. It is this "pin code" that opens the door of His throne and allows us to enter. Until you enter His Presence, your prayer will not be answered. Praying outside His Presence leads to frustration because no result will be achieved, and this is the biggest frustration in the church today. Lots of believers are praying, but answers are not coming because they pray amiss. At the end, they give up with the conclusion that God does not answer all prayers. But the truth is that God answers prayers that are prayed according to His principles. Jesus taught His disciples these principles when they asked Him to teach them how to pray.

> *And it came to pass that as He was praying in a certain place, when He ceased, one of His disciples said unto Him, "Lord, teach us to pray as John also taught his disciples."*

And He said unto them, "When ye pray, say: Our Father who art in Heaven, hallowed be Thy name......
—Luke 11:1-2

In the above verses, Jesus gave His disciples the "pin code" of entering into God's Presence, and that "pin code" is reverence for God. "Our Father, hallowed be thy name" means "Our Father, holy is your name." It takes the reverence of God's name to enter into His Presence. How do we revere his name?

We start first with ourselves, by clearly examining ourselves, to see if we are clean to appear before the Holy God. The Bible says in Psalm 24:3-5 that only those with clean heart are permitted into the hills of the Lord, meaning His Presence.

Who shall ascend onto the hill of the Lord? Or who shall stand in His Holy Place? He that hath clean hands and a pure heart, who hath not lifted up his soul unto vanity, nor sworn deceitfully.

He shall receive the blessing from the Lord, and righteousness from the God of his salvation. —Psalm 24:3-5

A person who reveres God will not rush into the Presence of the Holy God without first cleaning himself with the precious blood of Jesus. As long as we live in this body, we are not perfect. Therefore, in order to be allowed into His Presence, the first step is to clean up with His blood, from inside because only a pure heart can see Him (Matthew 5:8). Note that it takes holiness to see God (Hebrews 12:14). Both in the Old and New Testaments, God emphasized the reason to be holy before we see Him. That reason is because He is a Holy God. Therefore, for us to be able to approach His Presence, He wants us to be like Him in holiness. It is only the blood of Jesus that can cleanse us of all unrighteousness and present us holy like Him.

The blood of Jesus does not also give us the license to live any way we want just because we can always apply it to clean ourselves, just like many think and call it the era of grace. We must bear in mind that a sinful lifestyle hinders answers to prayer; therefore, we should make the decision to live right. Grace is not a license to sin and run under the blood of Jesus before we pray. We should live a holy life if we want to be allowed into the Presence of God. Secondly, I must emphasize that no matter how holy you may live, you are not going to be perfect; therefore, you still need the blood to cleanse you before you go into His Presence.

> *For I am the LORD your God. Ye shall therefore sanctify yourselves, and ye shall be holy, for I am holy; neither shall ye defile yourselves with any manner of creeping thing that creepeth upon the earth.* —Leviticus 11:44

> *And ye shall be holy unto Me; for I the LORD am holy and have severed you from other people, that ye should be Mine.* —Leviticus 20:26

> *But if we walk in the light, as He is in the light, we have fellowship one with another, and the blood of Jesus Christ His Son cleanseth us from all sin. If we say that we have no sin, we deceive ourselves and the truth is not in us. If we confess our sins, He is faithful and just to forgive us our sins, and to cleanse us from all unrighteousness. If we say that we have not sinned, we make Him a liar, and His Word is not in us.* —1 John 1:7-10

Because God unites with us when we pray, it is very important that we understand that He is a holy God and, therefore, He will not contaminate Himself with our sinful life style; that is why it is necessary for us to cleanse ourselves before we enter into His

Presence. The only thing that can clean us is the precious blood of Jesus as stated in 1 John 1:7-10.

Then you go into His Presence praising His Holy name (Hallow be thy Name). Praise brings us into the Presence of God. It is the key that opens the gates of His throne. It is the master key that invites God into our altar of prayer.

> *Enter into His gates with thanksgiving, and into His courts with praise! Be thankful unto Him, and bless His name. —Psalm 100:4*

Many Christians enter into prayer with complaints and never receive answers because that is a wrong way to enter into the presence of God. In short, angels will not allow you into the presence of God when you come with complaints. Complaining is murmuring and God hates to see His children murmur. When you complain or murmur, you are automatically saying that your situation is bigger than God. When the children of Israel murmured after God had supernaturally delivered them from Egypt, they incurred the wrath of God because murmuring is equal to unbelief and God hates when His children doubt Him.

> *How long shall I bear with this evil congregation who murmur against Me? I have heard the murmurings of the children of Israel, which they murmur against Me. Say unto them, 'As truly as I live, saith the LORD, as ye have spoken in Mine ears, so will I do to you. Your carcasses shall fall in this wilderness; and all who were numbered of you, according to your whole number, from twenty years old and upward, who have murmured against Me, doubtless ye shall not come into the land concerning which I swore to make you dwell therein, save Caleb the son of Jephunneh and Joshua the son of Nun. But your little ones, whom ye*

> *said should be a prey, them will I bring in, and they shall know the land which ye have despised. But as for you, your carcasses, they shall fall in this wilderness. And your children shall wander in the wilderness forty years and bear your whoredoms, until your carcasses be wasted in the wilderness.*
>
> *After the number of the days in which ye searched the land, even forty days, for each day a year, shall ye bear your iniquities, even forty years, and ye shall know My altering of My purpose. I, the LORD, have said: I will surely do it unto all this evil congregation who are gathered together against Me. In this wilderness they shall be consumed, and there they shall die.* — Numbers 14:27-35

The Israelites forfeited the promise of entering into the promise land because of complains and murmuring. Likewise today, many Christians are forfeiting their inheritance because they go into prayer with complains, crying and self-sympathy and were never allowed into the Presence of God by the angels. Therefore, all the hours spent in the "supposed" prayers were in vain. And the funniest thing is that they continue that way year in and year out until they are frustrated and give up praying and thereby forfeiting their promises.

God dwells in our praises; He loves it when we come into His presence with praises and thanksgiving. It is praise that invites Him into our altar of prayer to fellowship with us. And when He comes, He initiates worship which is the answer that He accepted our praises. Worship glorifies Him and draws us deeper into His Presence for close fellowship and communion. When we come deeper into His Presence, communion, which is prayer, becomes very effective and an answer is certain.

God initiates worship; it is the answer that God gives in response to your praises. He is the one that initiates worship, which declares who He is; worship brings you deeper into His Presence to be anointed. When this happens, joy, peace and rest take place in your spirit, which ignites boldness and faith to declare His Word.

> *O how great is Thy goodness which Thou hast laid up for them that fear Thee, which Thou hast wrought for them that trust in Thee before the sons of men! Thou shalt hide them in the safety of Thy presence from the pride of man; Thou shalt keep them secretly in a pavilion from the strife of tongues.* —Psalm 31:19-20

> *He that dwelleth in the secret place of the Most High shall abide under the shadow of the Almighty. I will say of the LORD, "He is my refuge and my fortress; my God, in Him will I trust." Surely He shall deliver thee from the snare of the fowler and from the noisome pestilence. He shall cover thee with His feathers, and under His wings shalt thou trust; His truth shall be thy shield and buckler. Thou shalt not be afraid of the terror by night, nor of the arrow that flieth by day, nor of the pestilence that walketh in darkness, nor of the destruction that layeth waste at noonday.*

> *A thousand shall fall at thy side, and ten thousand at thy right hand, but it shall not come nigh thee. Only with thine eyes shalt thou behold and see the reward of the wicked. Because thou hast made the LORD, who is my refuge, even the Most High, thy habitation, there shall no evil befall thee, neither shall any plague come nigh thy dwelling.* —Psalm 91:1-10

It is only in His presence that the evil one has no access—only the righteous has access into His Presence. It is where boldness is imputed, anointing to declare and possess is ignited in our spirits.

It is not a place of warfare because no demon has entrance into the Presence of the Most High. It is a place reserved for those who are in Christ Jesus and walk righteously. It is a place we receive answers and minister answers to the needy. It is only in His Presence that we are anointed to pray a prayer that never fails. When the anointing rests upon you, then you are ready to pray a prayer that is devastating to the kingdom of darkness. In this place all kinds of prayers, such as supplication, intercession, dedication, consecration, etc., are effectively offered. If it is supplication, declare the promises you are expecting God to answer, and if it is intercession, allow the Holy Spirit to pray through you.

> *Fret not about anything, but in everything, by prayer and supplication with thanksgiving, let your requests be made known unto God. And the peace of God, which passeth all understanding, shall keep your hearts and minds through Christ Jesus.* —Philippians 4:6

Fretting about our needs comes as a result of doubt. Many are not sure if they will receive answers and that uncertainty is wiped out when you are in the Presence of your father who has promised to give as you ask. Because of His Presence, your confidence will be restored and you will be quite assured that He will answer because it is now mouth to mouth communication in His Holy of Holies.

If it is intercession you are doing, allow the Holy Spirit to intercede on behalf of the saints through you. Why? You may not know what the person or persons are passing through, so allow Him who knows to pray through you. It is a communication between God the Spirit and God the Father. Let me make this clear, when God the Spirit communicates with God the Father, there is 100% certainty that the deal is done. That is why He was sent to you and me to help us pray and also reveal to us what the outcome of His communication with the Father is.

Likewise the Spirit also helpeth our infirmities; for we know not what we should pray for as we ought, but the Spirit itself maketh intercession for us with groanings which cannot be uttered. And He that searcheth the hearts knoweth what is the mind of the Spirit, because He maketh intercession for the saints according to the will of God. And we know that all things work together for good to those who love God, to those who are the called according to His purpose. —Romans 8:26-28

Praying always with all prayer and supplication in the Spirit, and watching thereunto with all perseverance and supplication for all saints. And pray for me, that utterance may be given unto me, that I may open my mouth boldly to make known the mystery of the Gospel. —Ephesians 6:18-19

But as it is written: "Eye hath not seen, nor ear heard, neither have entered into the heart of man the things which God hath prepared for them that love Him." But God hath revealed them unto us by His Spirit. For the Spirit searcheth all things, yea, the deep things of God. —1 Corinthians 2:9-10

However when He, the Spirit of Truth, is come, He will guide you into all truth; for He shall not speak from Himself, but whatsoever He shall hear, that shall He speak; and He will show you things to come. He shall glorify me, for He shall receive of Mine, and shall show it unto you. —John 16:13-14

After you have prayed before His Presence, the next step is to be silent in His Presence in order to hear from Him. Many of us fail in this place because we like to only talk, talk and talk without listening to whom we are talking to. God wants to speak to us in response to our prayer. It is His answer that directs or instructs us on how the answers to our prayers can manifest. Therefore, it is very important that we practice listening because if you don't hear, you may not know what to do. In this moment of silence, you give God the opportunity to speak to you either by a still small voice, vision or trance. It might take a long or short time, but decide to wait until He speaks because that is what prayer is all about. It is communication with God. When you were speaking for 30 minutes, one hour or two hours, He kept quiet to hear from you. So learn the same way to be quiet in order to hear from Him.

> *Be silent, O all flesh, before the LORD, for He is raised up out of His holy habitation.* —Zechariah 2:13

> *Be still, and know that I am God; I will be exalted among the heathen, I will be exalted on the earth.* — Psalm 46:10

> *On the morrow, as they went on their journey and drew nigh unto the city, Peter went up upon the housetop to pray about the sixth hour. And he became very hungry and would have eaten; but while they were making ready he fell into a trance, and saw heaven opened and a certain vessel descending unto him as though it had been a great sheet knit at the four corners and let down to the earth, wherein were all kinds of four-footed beasts of the earth, and wild beasts and creeping things and fowls of the air.*

> *And there came a voice to him, "Rise, Peter; kill and eat."*

> *But Peter said, "Not so, Lord, for I have never eaten anything that is common or unclean."*

And the voice spoke unto him again the second time, "What God hath cleansed, that call not thou common."

This was done thrice, and the vessel was received up again into heaven.

*Now while Peter wondered to himself what this vision which he had seen could mean, behold, the men who had been sent from Cornelius had made inquiry for Simon's house and stood before the gate. —*Acts 10:9-17

In the above story in Acts 10, we see that Peter went to pray and by trance, the Lord spoke to Him. Peter did not walk away and say, "What are all these reptiles?" No, he waited in His Presence and as He waited the voice came and interpreted to Him what the Lord meant. It was not recorded how long he waited but the Bible says he waited while food was been prepared. You can agree with me that food preparation in those days took longer than our modern electric and gas cookers. If we are going to be effective in our prayers, we must learn to wait on the Lord to hear from Him. And when we hear, no matter how unreasonable it may sound or look, we must learn to act on what He says. It was unreasonable for Peter to go and associate with the Gentiles being a Jew. But Peter laid down his reasons and went with the servants of Cornelius. Your action to what He said is what brings the manifestation to what you ask. After you have heard, chose to act in faith by praising Him. Your praise is a proof that you believe what He spoke to you. It is your praise that causes the manifestation.

(As it is written: "I have made thee a father of many nations"), in the presence of Him whom he believed, even God, who quickeneth the dead and calleth those things which are not, as though they were.

Abraham, against all hope, believed in hope, that he might become the father of many nations, according to that which had been spoken, "So shall thy seed be."

And being not weak in faith, he considered not his own body now dead, when he was about a hundred years old, nor yet the deadness of Sarah's womb.

He staggered not at the promise of God through unbelief, but was strong in faith, giving glory to God, and being fully persuaded that what He had promised, He was able also to perform. —Romans 4:19-21

Let the people praise Thee, O God; let all the people praise Thee. Then shall the earth yield her increase; and God, even our own God, shall bless us. God shall bless us, and all the ends of the earth shall fear Him. —Psalm 67:5-7

Our praise when we hear His voice is a strong proof to the devil that you believe God despite what may be happening around you. This is the key that brings down what is in the spirit to the physical realm, thus fulfilling our joy. Read this testimony.

In 2011, my wife and I sowed a seed of $6428 into the ministry of Dr. Morris Cerullo of San Diego, California; as a seed for a desired home. We made a vow in January 2011 and completed the sowing of the seed in May 2011 and went out to look for a home. We found a beautiful home of our desire in our neighborhood. When we asked the price of this home, it was so much, but immediately we had favor from the owner by reducing the price by $ 124,725. With this, the first bank we approached agreed to sponsor the buying of the home 100% seeing that the value of the house was higher than the price the owner was giving to us. All documents were submitted and when the final decision was taken, the bank changed their mind and asked us to make a down payment of $137,362. This final decision was taken on the June 24, 2011, the day we had our monthly all-night prayer meeting. I was disappointed and did not feel like going to the prayer meeting. But after I spoke to the owner of the house, he was also disappointed and called an estate agent who had someone with cash to buy the house. So I was sad, but I decided to go to the all-night prayer.

We had a good time in His Presence. At about 4:00am, in the early morning of June 25, we were ending our prayer and we all went into worship for about half an hour, and there was silence, real silence, in His Presence. As we all knelt before His Presence, I went into trance and saw two of my dogs in this new home that the bank denied us. Then I heard a voice say, "What do you see?" I said, "My dogs in that house," and the voice came back, "That is your home; when you leave this prayer meeting, take anointing oil and anoint the gate of that home and claim it—it is yours," and the vision left.

I was wondering like Peter, because I know that going to that house at 5:00 am to anoint the gate was very risky. Why? The house is just three houses from the former governor of my Island and there was 24-hour security patrol in the street. But I decided to obey the voice of the Lord and drove straight to the gate of that home. The moment I finished anointing it, I opened my car to enter and I saw the security patrol coming. I thought *Praise God; mission is already accomplished.*

I then went the following week to meet my family on holiday in Europe. We spent three weeks there and came back and met the house unsold. Later, the owner called us and explained that the estate agent did not show up as promised. We wrote him a letter that for now we cannot afford the house but we still trust God. When he got our letter, he invited us to talk again. My wife and I went and he asked me to try another bank. I sluggishly accepted to try another bank. Fortunately, the first bank I entered, I saw that the receptionist is a member of our church. She introduced me to a very kind accountant.

At the end of our discussion, I was informed to make a down payment of $76,923. I went back and informed my wife whose faith was so strong that if God revealed that the house is ours, He will provide. So we called the owner of the house and made an appointment again. In the meeting, he explained to us his frustration and the amount of money he was losing each day in the Island because he had sold his business and was planning another business in Europe. At the end he said, "This is what I will do: I will give you people the down payment free because calculating how much I am losing daily, it is better to pay this down payment for you people as far as you will buy the house and give me the cash. I want to leave." My wife and I looked at each other and could not believe what we heard. At the end, he paid that money into the Notary's account and we signed and finally bought the house, thus fulfilling what the Lord revealed to me when we were silently waiting in His Presence. Here is the picture of the home.

Shalom.

CHAPTER FOUR

The Place of Obedience

The place of obedience in answered prayers cannot be denied. Indeed, if you want to receive answers to your prayers, you must make up your mind to obey the Word of God first or forget about wasting your precious time in prayer. I have seen many believers trying to bribe God into breaking His covenant and blessing them. God will never break His covenant as He promised in Psalm 89:34, and that is the reason you see those set of believers praying for one thing for 30 years and they continue thinking that one day God will answer. This is the terminology such people use often: "I am waiting for God." I always reply, "No dear, God is waiting for you." The ministry of prayer demands two things from anyone who needs answer from God: discipline and diligence in obedience. When you are not disciplined to obey the Word of God, God will not also listen to your word when you talk to Him; indeed, He will not come near to you when you pray. Disobedience drives Him far away from us. Satan was sent away from His Presence due to disobedience; Adam and Eve were also sent out of His Presence because of disobedience, and the children of Israel were denied entrance into the promise land because of disobedience. So why do many Christians pray and think that God is with them and He will answer them when they are in disobedience to His Word? The answer is found in Hosea 4:6.

> *My people are destroyed for lack of knowledge. Because thou hast rejected knowledge, I will also reject thee, that thou shalt be no priest to Me. Seeing thou hast forgotten the law of thy God, I will also forget thy children.* —Hosea 4:6

Satan understands very well what disobedience will do to us, which is why he lures many to disobey God. Disobedience dethroned him and chased him away from God's Presence. He knows that if he can lure or deceive you to disobey God, your communion with Him will be cut off just like he did to Adam and Eve. If Adam and Eve knew that their communion with God would be cut off, they could not have chosen to go against the Word of God. That is why the Bible is written to teach us, so that we can escape every deceit of Satan, but because many do not read or study the Bible, they are still falling into the deceits of the enemy and Satan is making use of their ignorance to keep them in bondage.

> *And unto Adam He said, "Because thou hast hearkened unto the voice of thy wife, and hast eaten of the tree of which I commanded thee, saying, 'Thou shalt not eat of it,' cursed is the ground for thy sake; in sorrow shalt thou eat of it all the days of thy life. Thorns also and thistles shall it bring forth to thee, and thou shalt eat the herb of the field. In the sweat of thy face shalt thou eat bread till thou return unto the ground, for out of it wast thou taken; for dust thou art, and unto dust shalt thou return.* —Genesis 3:17-19

> *Therefore, the* LORD *God sent him forth from the Garden of Eden to till the ground from whence he was taken. So He drove out the man; and He placed at the east of the Garden of Eden cherubims and a flaming*

> *sword which turned every way, to keep the way of the tree of life.* —Genesis 3:23-24

> *For whatsoever things were written in times past, were written for our learning, that we through patience and comfort of the Scriptures might have hope.* —Romans 15:4

Disobedience drove them away from their blessing and they started to struggle in order to live. That is what the sweat means. Many Christians who are supposed to be living by faith in obedience to the Word of God and enjoying the fruit of obedience, which is blessing, are sweating today. And the funniest aspect of it is that the same group of Christians is running from one church to another or from one ministry or conference to another looking for men and women of God who will pray them out of sweating. They have been doing this for years and the result is frustration upon frustration. The simple truth is found in the above scriptures in Romans 15:4. All these were written for our learning, and it is very simple. God hates disobedience, and if He has written it down in numerous Bible verses, preached it to us through many preachers, and written it down through thousands of authors, it is time for us to grow up and do what is right so we can receive answers to our prayers. God does not hear the prayers of the disobedient. Look at the following scriptures for real confirmation.

> *Turn you at my reproof: Behold, I will pour out my spirit unto you; I will make known my words unto you. "Because I have called and ye refused, I have stretched out my hand and no man heeded, but ye have set at nought all my counsel and would have none of my reproof, I also will laugh at your calamity; I will mock when your fear cometh, when your fear cometh as desolation, and your destruction cometh*

as a whirlwind, when distress and anguish cometh upon you.

Then shall they call upon me, but I will not answer; they shall seek me early, but they shall not find me, because they hated knowledge, and did not choose the fear of the LORD. They would have none of my counsel, and they despised all my reproof: therefore shall they eat of the fruit of their own ways, and be filled with their own devices. —Proverbs 1:23-31

He that turneth away his ear from hearing the law, even his prayer shall be abomination. —Proverbs 28:9

When God directs you through His Word and you heed to the instruction and obey Him, then when you pray, angels stand still to hearken unto the voice of the commander in chief for the manifestation of answers to your prayers. Why? Because you do those things that pleases Him.

And whatsoever we ask we receive of Him, because we keep His commandment and do those things that are pleasing in His sight. —1 John 3:22

Are they not all ministering spirits, sent forth to minister for those who shall be heirs of salvation. — Hebrews 1:14

Bless the LORD, ye His angels that excel in strength, that do His commandments, hearkening unto the voice of His word. Bless ye the LORD, all ye His hosts, ye ministers of His, that do His pleasure. —Psalm 103:20-21

Until you do what is expected of you in the Word of God, your prayer to God is unaccepted. God performs His acts towards those who are in compliance with His instruction. In order to see quick answers to your prayers, you must decide to be diligent in obedience and discipline yourself towards obeying the Word of God. Prayer alone does not bring manifestation. Indeed, it is boldly written in the book of Deuteronomy 28 that when we diligently hearken to His voice, the end result is blessing. From here, I concluded years back that the obedience does not need much prayer for himself because His obedience speaks all the time before God. It is His obedience that gives him the boldness into the throne of God to demand what God has promised him. He knows that God is a covenant keeping God, and if he does his part, the God that cannot lie will definitely fulfill what He has promised. The obedient have confidence when they approach the throne of God because of walking the walk of righteousness. It is true that we are all righteous in Christ Jesus once we are born again, but we are requested to walk in light as He walked if we are going to enjoy the fruits of righteousness.

> *And it shall come to pass, if thou shalt hearken diligently unto the voice of the LORD thy God to observe and to do all His commandments which I command thee this day, that the LORD thy God will set thee on high above all nations of the earth; and all these blessings shall come on thee and overtake thee, if thou shalt hearken unto the voice of the LORD thy God: Blessed shalt thou be in the city, and blessed shalt thou be in the field. Blessed shall be the fruit of thy body, and the fruit of thy ground, and the fruit of thy herds, the increase of thy cattle, and the flocks of thy sheep. Blessed shall be thy basket and thy stores. Blessed shalt thou be when thou comest in, and blessed shalt thou be when thou goest out.* —Deuteronomy 28:1-6

God is not a man that He should lie; neither the son of man, that He should repent. Hath He said, and shall He not do it? Or hath He spoken, and shall He not make it good. —Numbers 23:19

In hope of eternal life, which God, who cannot lie, promised before the world began. —Titus 1:2

As a pastor, I have seen multitudes of Christians trying to convince God to bless them with tears at the altars of prayers. Many cry and mourn and tell God how much they love Him and they cannot imagine why He refused to bless them. Normally, some pastors will start to sympathize with this group of Christians, but sympathy does not move God to disobey His own Word. Indeed, if we look at the book of John chapter 14:21-24, we will discover that Jesus does not believe you love Him until you do what He says. Let us see that.

He that hath My commandments and keepeth them, he it is that loveth Me; and he that loveth Me shall be loved by My Father, and I will love him and will manifest Myself to him."

Judas (not Iscariot) said unto Him, "Lord, how is it that Thou wilt manifest Thyself unto us, and not unto the world?"

Jesus answered and said unto him, "If a man love Me, he will keep My words; and My Father will love him, and We will come unto him and make Our abode with him.

He that loveth Me not, keepeth not My sayings. And the Word which you hear is not Mine, but the Father's who sent Me. —John 14:21-24

When I discovered these scriptures, I made up my mind that before I ask God anything, I must check myself in His Word if I have obeyed what He said concerning what I am asking. Or when He speaks to me in a still small voice, if I have obeyed that voice. That was when answers to my prayers started manifesting very fast. So, I began to teach on obedience to the Word before prayer to our congregation with my personal testimonies. When they saw that truly it was not the devil that hindered their blessing but their disobedience, many of them turned from disobedience and started obeying the Word of God, and the result is the same as I have testified to them. These are few testimonies (both mine and others from our congregation).

At the end of the year 2009, I decided to fast for three days for personal and family matters mostly in the area of finance. So while I was praying, I told the Lord that I have read so many testimonies of people He gave financial breakthroughs in thousands and millions of dollars and I am also expecting Him to give me and my family financial breakthrough since we were doing His will. Then the Lord replied to me immediately and asked me to open my Bible to the book of 2 Corinthians 9:6. I opened it quickly and read it.

> *But this I say: He who soweth sparingly shall reap also sparingly, and he who soweth bountifully shall reap also bountifully.* —2 Corinthians 9:6

The Lord went further and said, "If you want to reap thousands, start to sow in thousand." Then my eyes were really opened to the scripture because my family and I have been sowing financial seeds since we became Christians, but we usually sowed in $100, $50 and $25 and the harvest had also been coming in hundreds of dollars. Below are evidence of our seed receipts since 1996.

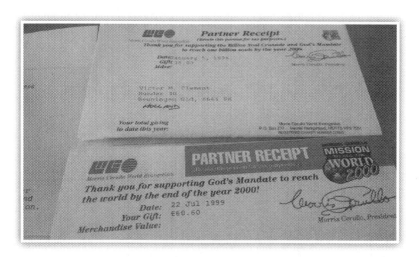

Partner Receipt

Thank you for supporting the Billion Soul Crusade and God's Mandate to reach one billion souls by the year 2000.

Date: January 5, 1996
Gift: 35.00
Misc:

Morris Cerullo, President

Victor M. Clement
Bunder 30
Beuningen GLd, 6641 SK

Your total giving
to date this year:

Morris Cerullo World Evangelism
P.O. Box 277 · Hemel Hempstead, HERTS HP2 7DH
REGISTERED CHARITY NUMBER 1003

PARTNER RECEIPT

MISSION WORLD 2000

Morris Cerullo World Evangelism

Thank you for supporting God's Mandate to reach
the world by the end of the year 2000!

Date: 22 Jul 1999
Your Gift: £60.60
Merchandise Value:

Morris Cerullo, President

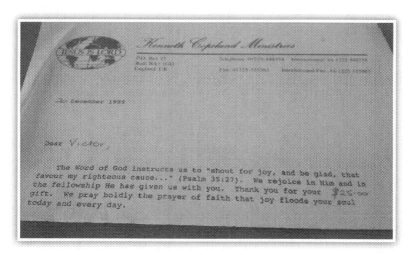

Kenneth Copeland Ministries

P.O. Box 15
Bath BA1 (UK)
England U.K.

Telephone 01225 345424 · International 44 1225 345424
Fax 01225 350061 · International Fax 44 1225 350061

30 December 1995

Dear Victor,

The Word of God instructs us to "shout for joy, and be glad, that favour my righteous cause..." (Psalm 35:27). We rejoice in Him and in the fellowship He has given us with you. Thank you for your $25.00 gift. We pray boldly the prayer of faith that joy floods your soul today and every day.

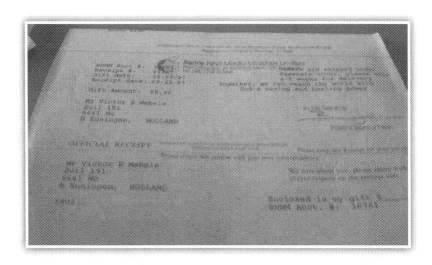

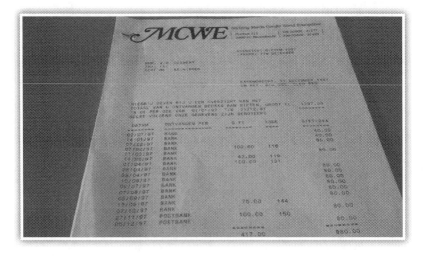

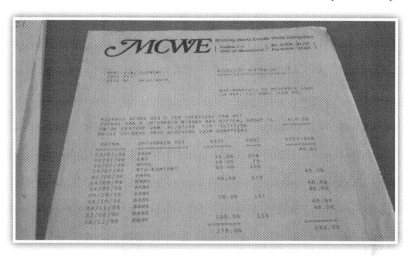

Image 8 is one of our files for the receipt of our offerings and tithes since August 1995, the same month I was born again. God is faithful to His Word. Many Christians groan and mourn that they are not seeing the fruit of their seed just like I did. Until the revelation behind small and big harvest was given to me; and the moment we decided to obey what the Lord had revealed, we discovered that God had been answering our prayers, but we were hindering our harvest by the quantity and quality of seed we sowed in the Kingdom.

The moment I came out from my prayer room, I made up my mind to start to sow seeds in thousands. I told my wife and we agreed. We knew it would be a sacrifice, but we decided to leave the level and start giving in the thousands. Few days after this incident, I was watching a live broadcast of Dr. Morris Cerullo from World Evangelism in Orlando during the first week of January 2010. Dr. Todd was teaching. So he called for people to sow a seed of $2010 representing the year 2010. In my spirit, there was joy of opportunity to sow, but I had only $260 in my pocket. So I made the vow online and sent out the $260 the same day. While in prayer two days later, the Lord said to me, "I am opening a closed door for a financial breakthrough because of the step of faith you made. So expect it." The moment I came out of my prayer room, my telephone rang and it was my lawyer. He had been handling an accident case for me since 2008 and the insurance company had refused to pay our claim of $16,483.51. So when he called, he said, "I have changed our claim to $32,967.03 because there were lots of mistakes during the procedure of your documents at the insurance company."

I said, "If they refused to pay half of what you are claiming now, how are you sure they will agree with your claim now?"

He replied, "Because I am ready to take them to court."

Immediately the Lord said to me, "Keep quiet and let him do his job."

Two hours later, he called back and demanded that I come quickly to his office. When I got there, he brought out a file with an agreement with the insurance company's director to settle the case amicably by paying the $32,967.03. He asked me to sign and I did. It was like a dream, but it was real. The moment I stepped out of his office, the Lord said, "This is the beginning; remember to pay your tithe and fulfill your vow to Dr. Morris Cerullo." I collected my cheque a few days later, paid my tithe and my vow and also sowed more seeds in thousands of dollars.

The same month, my wife and I received a scholarship of $52,000 for our PhD programs. What happened? When we obey God's

Word, 2 Corinthians 9:6 is fulfilled. The following year, I went personally to Dr. Morris Cerullo's World conference, sowed $2011 and made a vow of $4237 to the ministry. My wife and I fulfilled this vow at the end of May 2011, and the seed was named after our home. We were looking for a new home. By end of September 2011, the Lord provided money for us to acquire a beautiful home. Prayer can only work when it is accompanied with obedience.

Testimony of Mr. and Mrs. A:

This couple is members of our church. When they heard our testimonies of sowing seeds in thousands, they took the same step. The husband met me after a church service while we were preparing for one of our annual conferences. He handed an envelope to me and said, "This is for the conference." When I opened it, it was a thousand seed. Few days after that, I was at the hotel, making arrangements for the preachers and we were short on money. The wife called and asked to meet me at the hotel lobby. She came and handed over a thousand seed to me, which helped to offset our bill. Then after the conference, I went to the mother of her husband to pray for her and the husband took me to an empty land behind the parent's house and asked me to pray for favor for the finance to build their home. The moment I wanted to pray, the Lord spoke to me and asked me to take the anointing oil in my car and pour it on the empty ground and then declare favor. I obeyed and after six months, this home replaced the empty ground. Mr. and Mrs. Felicia prayed and obeyed and the result is this home.

Testimony of Mr. and Mrs. B:

When Mrs. B. came to our church in 2009, she was not yet married, jobless and very sick. She was born and raised in a Pentecostal church but never lived victoriously as a Christian until she came to our congregation. She started to hear the message of obedience and prayer and God healed and delivered her from all her troubles, gave her a permanent job and then she got married in 2013. She and her husband heard our testimonies and decided to obey God in sowing bountifully. At the end of 2014, the Lord provided for them to pay off their car and they bought the house below. This proved that obedience is one of the keys to answered prayers.

Testimony of Mr. and Mrs. C:

Mr. and MrsC. came to our church as visitors in late 2009 and became members on the January 14, 2010. They were a family of five with three children, and they had a small pick-up that could carry only two passengers and the driver. So you can imagine how they came to church in that pick-up. My prayer for them was for God to meet their need for a comfortable family car. They heard our testimonies and they learned that the key to prayer was obedience. In one of our conferences, they brought a seed of thousand and gave it to me as a support for the conference. They are very consistent tithers with their children. Not very long after the one thousand seed offering, God provided for them to buy the car below with cash, not via a loan from the bank. Right now as I am writing this book, their own house is being constructed. Below is also a picture of their house.

Testimony of Miss D.

Miss D and her mother were the first group of people that started at our house fellowship that grew to become our church. They have been so faithful in all they do in the church. The mother had a small car, but I never knew the condition of that car. First, when Miss D. graduated from college, she applied for a job in one of the leading firms in the island. The day she was going for interview, she called me worried that they would not employ her because in order to work in such place, you must know one of the top government officials or an influential person in society. We prayed and I told her that she knew the most influential person in the whole universe: Jesus Christ of Nazareth. She went and the procedure that was supposed to take at least two weeks took only 24 hours: she got the job! On this faithful day, my wife was supposed to pick me up at the radio station where our church has a weekly program and Miss D. is my translator; I decided to follow Miss D. and her mother in their car, so I told my wife to wait for me at the church where she was having practice with the praise team. When I entered the car, I was shocked because of the condition of the car. I was angry inside because I know how obedient they were in giving and serving the church. I got home, went into my prayer room and started interceding for a financial breakthrough for them. Then the Lord answered and said, "I have made a way for them because of their obedience and faithfulness." A few weeks after this incident, Miss D. bought the Kia Sportage below. Assuming they were not in obedience, I would not have had the boldness to go before God to intercede. It was their obedience that "fueled' my passion to go into intercession on their behalf and God demonstrated the power of obedience in our prayers by making a way for them to have a new car.

Testimony of Mrs. E.

Mrs. E. is the oldest woman in our church. She is 78 years old. She is a great intercessor for me, my family and the church. She comes to every prayer meeting despite her age. A few years ago, she started to sow seed of $55 every month into my life. One day as I was praying, I was led by the Holy Spirit to pray for a new car for her because her old car was giving her trouble. At her age, no bank would give her a loan, so it must be supernatural. A few weeks after that, a family member called her and bought a new car for her. That is the car below.

Looking at this, she had no money to buy a new car, but she understood the power of seed and prayer as she listened to our testimonies and messages on prayer and obedience. We cannot separate obedience from prayer—they are like twins. If you are in obedience to the Word of God as you read these testimonies, do not give up; hold onto your faith because if God did it for these people, He will surely do it for you because He is not a respecter of persons. If you are receiving breakthrough but not enough to meet your needs, make a step of faith like the testimonies you have read and watch God to do the same for you.

> *Then Peter opened his mouth and said, "In truth I perceive that God is no respecter of persons, but in every nation he that feareth Him and worketh righteousness is accepted by Him.* —Acts 10:34-35

It also takes obedience to deal with demonic powers and imaginations that raises themselves against the knowledge of truth. Many Christians have fallen into trouble because they tried to deal with demonic powers in warfare prayer when they were not in obedience to the Word of God. When we live in obedience, God gives us His backing to deal with the power of darkness. Many of us quote 2 Corinthians 10:3-5 and omit verse 6, whereas it is impossible to pull down strongholds when your obedience is not completed.

> *For though we walk in the flesh, we do not war according to the flesh. For the weapons of our warfare are not carnal, but mighty through God for the pulling down of strongholds, casting down imaginations and every high thing that exalteth itself against the knowledge of God, and bringing into captivity every thought to the obedience of Christ, and being in readiness to avenge all disobedience when your obedience is fulfilled.* —2 Corinthians 10:3-6

When our obedience is completed, whatever we declare, God will bring it to pass. A story in the book of Acts 19 is very interesting. Let us read it together.

> *And God wrought special miracles by the hands of Paul, so that handkerchiefs or aprons from his body were brought unto the sick, and the diseases departed from them and the evil spirits went out of them.*

Then certain of the vagabond Jews, exorcists, took it upon themselves to pronounce the name of the Lord Jesus over those who had evil spirits, saying, "We adjure you by Jesus whom Paul preacheth."

And there were seven sons of one Sceva, a Jew and chief of the priests, who did so. And the evil spirit answered and said, "Jesus I know, and Paul I know, but who are ye?"

And the man in whom the evil spirit dwelt leaped on them, and overcame them, and prevailed against them, so that they fled out of that house naked and wounded. —Acts 19:11-16

Paul lived in obedience, so when he invoked the name of Jesus, Heaven confirmed his word. But the sons of Sceva tried to use the same name, but failed because their obedience was not completed as stated in 2 Corinthians 10:6. I found out here that demons know when you are living right and when you are not living right, they will ask, "Who are you to cast us out while you are in our class, we know those that have right to cast us out," (paraphrased).

I believe that your faith is made strong right now after reading these testimonies. We have a lot of stories and I am looking forward to adding yours to the next edition of this book. Shalom.

CHAPTER FIVE

The Place of the Holy Spirit in Prayer

He is the Spirit of prayer, our intercessor, the one that prays the mysteries out. He is the one that prays when we do not know what to pray or how to offer our petition before the throne of grace. He is the one that picks us up and works through us when we are weak. Until we allow Him to pray through us, we will not know the true meaning and depth of prayer. He was sent to us to help us pray and to fulfill our Christian race on Earth. Without Him, there is no Christianity but religion. He is the all-knowing; He is God on Earth today. It is His power that sets our prayers ablaze to deal with every demonic power that has kept men, societies and nations in bondage. He is the Spirit of supplication.

> *But ye shall receive power after the Holy Ghost is come upon you; and ye shall be witnesses unto Me both in Jerusalem, and in all Judea and in Samaria, and unto the uttermost part of the earth. —Acts 1:8*

> *Likewise, the Spirit also helpeth our infirmities; for we know not what we should pray for as we ought, but the Spirit itself maketh intercession for us with groanings which cannot be uttered.*

And He that searcheth the hearts knoweth what is the mind of the Spirit, because He maketh intercession for the saints according to the will of God. And we know that all things work together for good to those who love God, to those who are the called according to His purpose. —Romans 8:26-28

However, I am telling you nothing but the truth when I say it is profitable (good, expedient, advantageous) for you that I go away. Because if I do not go away, the Comforter (Counselor, Helper, Advocate, Intercessor, Strengthener, Standby) will not come to you [into close fellowship with you]; but if I go away, I will send Him to you [to be in close fellowship with you]. —John 16:7 *(Amplified Bible)*

Praying in the Spirit helps us to reinforce our prayer. It helps us to confront the forces of darkness in the spirit realm, as our flesh is unequal with these forces. True breakthrough in prayer is only possible when we allow the Spirit of God to pray through us. There are forces beyond our human ability in prayer; therefore, in order to engage and subdue these forces, it will take a higher power than them, and the only power above them is the power of the Holy Spirit. In Ephesians 6, the Holy Spirit revealed these powers through Paul's writing to the church of Ephesus.

Finally, my brethren, be strong in the Lord and in the power of His might. Put on the whole armor of God, that ye may be able to stand against the wiles of the devil. For we wrestle not against flesh and blood, but against principalities, against powers, against the rulers of the darkness of this world, against spiritual wickedness in high places.

> *Therefore, take unto you the whole armor of God, that ye may be able to withstand in the evil day and, having done all, to stand. Stand therefore, having your loins girded about with truth, and having on the breastplate of righteousness, and your feet shod with the preparation of the Gospel of peace.*
>
> *Above all, take the shield of faith, wherewith ye shall be able to quench all the fiery darts of the wicked. And take the helmet of salvation and the sword of the Spirit, which is the Word of God, praying always with all prayer and supplication in the Spirit, and watching thereunto with all perseverance and supplication for all saints.* —Ephesians 6:10-18

God has clothed us with all His armor and filled us with His Spirit to deal with all these powers. When you pray in the Spirit, you are simply allowing God the Spirit to talk to God the Father on your behalf. Let it be assured that when God is handling your affair in the spirit realm, victory is sure. The Bible says that when we pray in the spirit, we do not understand but God does, and He prays His perfect will for us. He prays the mysteries of God, which He later reveals to us that we might understand all He communicated with the Father on our behalf.

> *For he that speaketh in an unknown tongue speaketh not unto men, but unto God, for no man understandeth him, however it may be that in the spirit he speaketh mysteries.* —1 Corinthians 14:2
>
> *But as it is written: "Eye hath not seen, nor ear heard, neither have entered into the heart of man the things which God hath prepared for them that love Him."*

But God hath revealed them unto us by His Spirit. For the Spirit searcheth all things, yea, the deep things of God.

For what man knoweth the things of a man, save the spirit of man which is in him? Even so no man knoweth the things of God, but the Spirit of God.

Now we have received, not the spirit of the world, but the Spirit which is of God, that we might know the things that are freely given to us by God. —1 Corinthians 2:9-12

When we pray in the Spirit, we allow God-to-God communication on our behalf to take place, and the end result is always the perfect will of God in our lives. When we allow the Holy Spirit to pray for us, we overcome the weakness of our flesh as stated in Romans 8:26. It takes us far above what our human strength can reach in prayer. Many Christians have limited their lives by refusing to allow the Spirit of God to intercede for them. He is our help when we don't know what to pray or how to pray it. Many Christians are weak in prayer, and that is when we should allow Holy Spirit to help us overcome the human flesh, take us into Heaven frequently and receive from the Father what He has hidden for us and not from us. Many have also died in warfare because they did not know what they were confronting; but assuming they allowed the Holy Spirit to pray for them, He could have been able to use the spiritual hammer of God to deal with those forces and give us victory.

In the year 1997, I was under a heavy attack from a wizard who was in control of my family. This man made himself the god of my family. He so held them in bondage that whatever he said was the final decision. I called my mother and told her to stop taking my name to him to protect me through witchcraft, but it was too late because he already had my name in his demonic altar. He knew I was the only person that could stop him in the name of Jesus and, therefore, he decided to eliminate me through enchantment.

> *Surely there is no enchantment against Jacob, neither is there any divination against Israel. According to this time it shall be said of Jacob and of Israel, "What hath God wrought!"* —Numbers 23:23

The whole of my body was in pain and I could not turn my neck. I went to the doctor, my pastor came and prayed for me, but all were in vain; rather the pain increased every day. It got to the stage where I became angry and asked the Lord to take me to Heaven because I was tired of the pain. The same evening I prayed for death, I saw myself walking out of my body towards my door. And when I looked back to my bed, I saw my body lying down and a big snake tied round my neck. Immediately I saw a big hand that held the snake by the head and threw it away, then the hand pointed at me and immediately I came back into my body and the pains were instantly gone. I was shocked after all of this happened, but I knew that the Lord had delivered me from my enemies. *Who is behind this act?* was the question in my mind. The same night, I was a little weak but healed totally, then all of a sudden I perceived a demonic sensation in my room and I heard the Lord speak softly, "Pray in the spirit." I started praying in the spirit immediately and all my weakness was gone within 15 minutes and I transitioned into real spiritual warfare prayer for about two hours. At the end of praying in the spirit, a vision came up immediately and I saw this wizard (the man controlling my maternal family) in my room with a two-edged knife attempting to stab me. But he could not come closer to me because out of my mouth was coming out Isaiah 54:17.

> *No weapon that is formed against thee shall prosper; and every tongue that shall rise against thee in judgment thou shalt condemn. This is the heritage of*

the servants of the LORD, *and their righteousness is of Me," saith the*LORD. —Isaiah 54:17

Then the man moved back and spread his two hands, which automatically turned into two big wings. Then I shouted in the vision, "So you are the wizard after my life"; then I moved back, knelt down and raised my hands towards Heaven and called, "Abba Father, the Blood, Abba Father, the Blood." Before I could finish calling the third time, I saw a hand from Heaven with a bow of blood poured upon this man. Before the blood got to him, it turned to fire and consumed him and the vision left. I was totally convinced that I had won the battle. So I picked up my phone and called one of my sisters whose husband introduced that wizard to our family. I told her boldly that the wizard would die soon and she called me a big mouth. Guess what? That man died at his altar while he was invoking curses and was found dead in his shrine. I said to myself and to the people around me that if not for the praying in the spirit that night, I could have been dead. And Listen, this enchantment was taking place back in Nigeria and I was living in Europe. This is the reason Jesus called the Word He spoke Spirit. Words are Spirit; you can affect situations in another continent from your prayer room in the US. Witchcraft understands this power of invoking cursed words upon people and nations, but many Christians are still living in ignorance because we have not allowed the Spirit of God to take us into the Spirit world through praying in the Spirit and to reveal to us what is taking place there.

> *It is the Spirit that quickeneth; the flesh profiteth nothing. The words that I speak unto you, they are spirit, and they are life.* —John 6:63

> *I, John, who also am your brother and companion in tribulation and in the Kingdom and patience of Jesus Christ, was on the isle that is called Patmos, for the*

> *Word of God and for the testimony of Jesus Christ.*
> *I was in the Spirit on the Lord's Day, and I heard*
> *behind me a great voice as of a trumpet.* —Revelation
> 1:9-10

For you to know, see and hear what is in the Spirit, you must be in the Spirit. One of the ways to be in the Spirit is to pray in the Spirit. You cannot understand what the spirit is or what is in the spirit when you are all the time carnal. Why? Carnality and God are enemies; this is why most carnal Christians can never experience their fullness in God or live victoriously. God wants us to live victoriously, and that is why He has given us His Spirit to teach us, pray for us and reveal to us His plans for our lives. It is a free gift to us; therefore, leave religion and embrace the Spirit of God and watch Him take you from glory to glory.

> *For those who are according to the flesh mind the*
> *things of the flesh; but those who are according to the*
> *Spirit, the things of the Spirit.*
>
> *For to be carnally minded is death, but to be spiritually*
> *minded is life and peace, because the carnal mind is*
> *enmity against God, for it is not subject to the law of*
> *God, neither indeed can be.*
>
> *So then, those who are in the flesh cannot please God.*
>
> *But ye are not in the flesh, but in the Spirit, if so it*
> *be that the Spirit of God dwell in you. Now if any*
> *man have not the Spirit of Christ, he is none of His.*
> —Romans 8:5-9
>
> *However, when He, the Spirit of Truth, is come, He*
> *will guide you into all truth; for He shall not speak*

from Himself, but whatsoever He shall hear, that shall He speak; and He will show you things to come. — John 16:13

But as it is written: "Eye hath not seen, nor ear heard, neither have entered into the heart of man the things which God hath prepared for them that love Him." But God hath revealed them unto us by His Spirit. For the Spirit searcheth all things, yea, the deep things of God. —1 Corinthians 2:9-10

In our congregation, we spend time praying in tongues, mostly in our early-hour prayer meetings that starts at 4:00 am. Wake up early like Jesus and allow the Holy Spirit to pray through you and reveal to you your daily activities before the sun rises.

And in the morning, rising up a great while before day, He went out and departed into a solitary place, and there prayed. —Mark 1:35

It takes discipline. Do it and live victoriously because that is God's will for you. Shalom.

CHAPTER SIX

Fasting and Importance of Fasting

Fasting is the voluntary abstention from food for a certain period of time to seek the face of God concerning the situation confronting you. The role of fasting is very vital in our prayers. Jesus emphasized on fasting after making reference to the importance of faith in our prayers. Fasting boosts or reinforces our prayer to deal with some resisting evil forces.

> *However this kind goeth not out but by prayer and fasting.* —Matthew 17:21

When fasting is combined with our prayers and faith in the Word of God, every resisting demon is bound to submit to you.

There are different kinds of fasting recorded in the Bible:

1. Total Fasting. This is abstention from food and water for a period of time. The book of Esther recorded that Esther and the Jews did this type of fasting when Haman tried to destroy the Jews.
2. Absolute Fasting. In this type of fasting, you abstain from eating solid food for a period of time, but you can drink water. This kind of fasting was recorded in Luke 4 where Jesus fasted 40 days.

3. Partial Fasting. In this type of fasting, certain foods are eliminated from your daily diet. This was recorded in the book of Daniel chapter 10.

In whichever kind of fasting we may adopt, one thing is very important: if you want to get results, then you must fast a God kind of fast. God has a way He requires us to fast that He might glorify His name through us. In Isaiah 58, God kind of fasting is recorded.

> *"Why have we fasted," say they, "and Thou seest not? Why have we afflicted our soul, and thou takest no note?" Behold, in the day of your fast ye find pleasure, and exact all your labors.*

> *Behold, ye fast for strife and debate, and to smite with the fist of wickedness; ye shall not fast as ye do this day, to make your voice to be heard on high.*

> *Is it such a fast that I have chosen? A day for a man to afflict his soul? Is it to bow down his head as a bulrush, and to spread sackcloth and ashes under him? Wilt thou call this a fast, and an acceptable day to the LORD?*

> *Is not this the fast that I have chosen: to loose the bands of wickedness, to undo the heavy burdens, and to let the oppressed go free, and that ye break every yoke?*

> *Is it not to deal thy bread to the hungry, and that thou bring the poor that are cast out to thy house?—when thou seest the naked, that thou cover him, and that thou hide not thyself from thine own flesh?*

> *Then shall thy light break forth as the morning, and thine health shall spring forth speedily; and*

> *thy righteousness shall go before thee; the glory of the* LORD*shall be thy rearward.*

> *Then shalt thou call, and the* LORD *shall answer; thou shalt cry, and He shall say, "Here I am." If thou take away from the midst of thee the yoke, the putting forth of the finger and speaking vanity, and if thou draw out thy soul to the hungry and satisfy the afflicted soul, then shall thy light rise in obscurity and thy darkness be as the noonday.*

> *And the* LORD *shall guide thee continually, and satisfy thy soul in drought, and make fat thy bones; and thou shalt be like a watered garden, and like a spring of water whose waters fail not.* —Isaiah 58:3-11

Many Christians fast the wrong way, and that is why few receive answers after fasting. When fasting is properly done according to how God stated in the above scriptures, victory is inevitable.

Fasting does not change God; it changes, conforms and releases power upon us to accomplish the will of God upon our lives. After Jesus fasted for 40 days, He came out full of power and His fame went abroad.

> *And Jesus, being full of the Holy Ghost, returned from the Jordan and was led by the Spirit into the wilderness, and for forty days was tempted by the devil. And in those days He ate nothing, and afterward when they were ended, He hungered. And Jesus returned in the power of the Spirit into Galilee, and His fame went out through all the region round about.* —Luke 4:1-2, 14

Fasting means denying the outer man physical food and feeding the inner man with the Word of God. And also set time apart within the period of fasting to talk to God and worship Him. When you do these things, your spirit man will be built up, which enables you to obtain results in the spirit realm and afterwards, the manifestation will take place in the physical realm. What happens when you fast is that your spiritual sensitivity is increased, so that you are able to receive instructions and directions from God on how to deal with issues facing you to obtain the desired results.

> *Moreover when ye fast, be not, as the hypocrites, of a sad countenance. For they disfigure their faces, that they may appear unto men to fast. Verily I say unto you, they have their reward. But thou, when thou fastest, anoint thine head and wash thy face, that thou appear not unto men to fast, but unto thy Father who is in secret; and thy Father, who seeth in secret, shall reward thee openly.* —Matthew 6:16-18

The Purposes of Fasting Are as Follows:

1. When fasting is done correctly, the will of God for you will be revealed. Fasting reveals the will and plans of God for us. Most of the time, when we are too much in the flesh, we cannot understand or know the will of God for us in whatever we want to do; it is very necessary then to abstain from food in this period and seek God to reveal to you His will, plan and purpose:

   > *It came to pass after this also, that the children of Moab and the children of Ammon, and with them others besides the Ammonites, came against Jehoshaphat to battle.*

> *Then there came some who told Jehoshaphat, saying, "There cometh a great multitude against thee from beyond the sea on this side of Syria; and behold, they are in Hazazontamar, which is Engedi."*

> *And Jehoshaphat feared, and set himself to seek the LORD, and proclaimed a fast throughout all Judah.....*

> *Then upon Jahaziel the son of Zechariah, the son of Benaiah, the son of Jeiel, the son of Mattaniah, a Levite of the sons of Asaph, came the Spirit of the LORD in the midst of the congregation.*

> *And he said, "Hearken ye, all Judah and ye inhabitants of Jerusalem, and thou King Jehoshaphat! Thus saith the LORD unto you: 'Be not afraid nor dismayed by reason of this great multitude; for the battle is not yours, but God's. Tomorrow go ye down against them. Behold, they come up by the cliff of Ziz, and ye shall find them at the end of the brook, before the Wilderness of Jeruel. Ye shall not need to fight in this battle. Set yourselves, stand ye still, and see the salvation of the LORD with you, O Judah and Jerusalem.' Fear not, nor be dismayed. Tomorrow go out against them, for the LORD will be with you.* —2 Chronicles 20:1-3, 14-17

When Judah fasted, God revealed to them his plans and as they acted in this plan, they got victory.

2. Fasting dethrones the Spirit of delay that hinders the manifestation of God's promises. There are forces of darkness in the spirit realm that fight against the kingdom of god consistently. Most of the time these forces hold back answers to our prayers and delay them in order to frustrate us and cause us

to accuse God. In Daniel chapter 10, God answered Daniel the moment Daniel prayed, but these forces held back the angel that was sent to deliver Daniel's answer. Daniel was able to overcome these powers because of fasting and prayer. While he continued to pray, reinforcement was taking place in the spirit realm and the enemy was defeated.

In the third year of Cyrus king of Persia a thing was revealed unto Daniel, whose name was called Belteshazzar. And the thing was true, but the time appointed was long; and he understood the thing, and had understanding of the vision.

In those days I, Daniel, was mourning three full weeks. I ate no pleasant bread, neither came flesh nor wine in my mouth, neither did I anoint myself at all, till three whole weeks were fulfilled. And behold, a hand touched me, which set me upon my knees and upon the palms of my hands.

And he said unto me, "O Daniel, a man greatly beloved, understand the words that I speak unto thee, and stand upright; for unto thee am I now sent." And when he had spoken this word unto me, I stood trembling.

Then said he unto me, "Fear not, Daniel, for from the first day that thou didst set thine heart to understand and to chasten thyself before thy God, thy words were heard; and I have come for thy words. But the prince of the kingdom of Persia withstood me one and twenty days; but lo, Michael, one of the chief princes, came to help me, and I remained there with the kings of Persia. Now I have come to make thee understand what shall

> *befall thy people in the latter days, for yet the vision is*
> *for many days."* —Daniel 10: 1-3, 10-14

When you are experiencing delay in what you have asked God after you have obeyed Him, add fasting to your prayers, so that God can reveal to you why the delay is taking place.

3. Fasting brings healing to our body: When we fast, anointing, which is the power of God, is released upon us. Anointing destroy yokes.

    > *And it shall come to pass in that day, that his burden*
    > *shall be taken away from off thy shoulder and his*
    > *yoke from off thy neck, and the yoke shall be destroyed*
    > *because of the anointing.* —Isaiah 10:27

4. Fasting releases God's blessings, both natural and spiritual. Fasting is a channel by which God pours His blessing upon our lives. When the children of Israel were mocked and ridiculed, God sent His prophet and announced fasting for the entire nation. They hearkened unto the voice of the Lord and God turned their reproach into blessing:

    > *Blow the trumpet in Zion, sanctify a fast! Call a solemn*
    > *assembly, gather the people! Sanctify the congregation,*
    > *assemble the elders, gather the children and those that*
    > *suck the breasts; let the bridegroom go forth from his*
    > *chamber and the bride out of her retreat. Let the priests,*
    > *the ministers of the* LORD, *weep between the porch*
    > *and the altar; and let them say, "Spare Thy people,*
    > *O* LORD, *and give not Thine heritage to reproach, that*
    > *the heathen should rule over them. Why should they*
    > *say among the people, 'Where is their God?'"*

*Then will the LORD be jealous for His land, and pity
His people. Yea, the LORD will answer and say unto
His people: "Behold, I will send you corn and wine
and oil, and ye shall be satisfied therewith; and I will
no more make you a reproach among the heathen…*

*Be glad then, ye children of Zion, and rejoice in the
LORD your God; for He hath given you the early rain
moderately, and He will cause to come down for you
the rain, the early rain and the latter rain in the
first month. And the floors shall be full of wheat, and
the vats shall overflow with wine and oil. And I will
restore to you the years that the locust hath eaten, the
cankerworm and the caterpillar and the palmer worm,
My great army which I sent among you.*

*And ye shall eat in plenty and be satisfied, and praise
the name of the LORD your God that hath dealt
wondrously with you; and My people shall never be
ashamed.*

*And ye shall know that I am in the midst of Israel, and
that I am the LORD your God, and none else; and My
people shall never be ashamed.*

*And it shall come to pass afterward that I will pour
out My Spirit upon all flesh; and your sons and your
daughters shall prophesy, your old men shall dream
dreams, your young men shall see visions.* —Joel 2:
15-19, 23-28

5. Fasting releases the power of God to do the work of God. It
is impossible for anyone to accomplish the purpose of God by
himself. When God calls, He anoints. It takes anointing, which

is His power, to fulfill His purpose on Earth. Fasting releases this power. After Jesus fasted for 40 days, He came out with power. If you are called into ministry by God and you want to see signs and wonders follow you, you must make up your mind to pay the price of consistent fasting.

And Jesus, being full of the Holy Ghost, returned from the Jordan and was led by the Spirit into the wilderness, and for forty days was tempted by the devil. And in those days He ate nothing, and afterward when they were ended, He hungered...

And Jesus returned in the power of the Spirit into Galilee, and His fame went out through all the region round about. —Luke 4:1-2, 14

In the year 2005, I had a visitation from the Lord in a vision. He took me to a gate that was closed and opened another gate. When I entered, it was the Island of Curacao. So the Lord asked me if I would go there and teach the people prayer. I said yes. He opened my hands and placed some golden coins and the vision left. By this time, I was an assistant pastor and the head of our intercessory department in our church in The Netherlands. So I told my wife the following morning and she explained to me that she had a similar vision two weeks prior but she decided not to tell me but prayed that the Lord Himself would reveal this to me. Why? By that time, I was busy preparing to migrate to US with the family. So, in December 2005, I visited the island with my pastor for eight days and I got acquainted with the island. In 2006, we started preparing to migrate to the Caribbean from Europe. We resigned our circular jobs, I closed my growing business and in January 13, 2007, we left Europe for Caribbean. But before we left, the Lord appeared to me again and instructed me to fast for 40 days when we arrived in Curacao. And He said that once I fast, in the last day of the 40 days fasting,

He will open a door for the island to hear my voice; and that will be the beginning of open doors for the church, which He will build through this mission. I obeyed and fasted 40 days and on the 40th day, a man called Norwin, now a pastor, came to visit me because he heard from my landlord that there was a missionary pastor in his house. When Pastor Norwin came, we had a great fellowship and he immediately invited me to his radio program in one of the leading radio stations in the island; thus, fulfilling what the Lord spoke to me in the second vision. After my first message in that radio station, doors were really opened and till today, we have recorded numerous miracles and breakthroughs at the Global House of Prayer, Curacao. There was a weekend the Lord asked me to fast for the Sunday service. He did not tell me why but He just instructed me to fast. I fasted and just in the middle of my sermon, a mad woman was dragged into the hall. She became violent towards her mother and two other relatives, who took her out of the psychiatrist hospital against the doctor's recommendation and brought her to church. Two of our ushers went to hold her and they were both beaten. As I watched the drama unfold, I understood why the Lord had asked me to fast. So I went closer and she turned towards me to fight. The only thing I said was, "In Jesus name," and she fell down at the altar and went to sleep instantly. I continued with my message. By this time, half of the congregation was already looking for a way to run out because a violent mad woman was in the church. So I calmed them down and the service continued while the mad women slept. At the end of the service, I called some intercessors around her, and laid my hands on her as we prayed. That was the end of her madness. Her parents took her home and after two days, one of our elders and I went to pay her a visit. When we saw her at the entrance of their home playing with her four-year-old daughter, we did not recognize that she was the woman who had been delivered two days prior. It was when we introduced ourselves that she said, "Are you the pastor that my mother brought me to?" I said yes, and then she hugged me and was full of joy. She has since 2007 gone back to work and till today, there is no longer any symptom of insanity both at home and at work. It was the fasting I did that released the power of God to deliver her that faithful day. Fasting reinforces the power of God in our lives. Shalom.

CHAPTER SEVEN

Stay in Praise, Thanksgiving and Patience until Manifestation

Praise is a weapon God has provided to His children for cheap victory. When you praise God in the midst of your circumstances, you automatically hand over that situation to God, and with any situation that God handles, victory is certain. The enemy knows this, which is why he sends some enemies of praise to hinder us from praising God. In the book of 2 Chronicles, the children of Israel with King Jehoshaphat employed the weapon of praise to manifest the answer that was given to them by God when they fasted and prayed.

> *It came to pass after this also, that the children of Moab and the children of Ammon, and with them others besides the Ammonites, came against Jehoshaphat to battle.*
>
> *Then there came some who told Jehoshaphat, saying, "There cometh a great multitude against thee from beyond the sea on this side of Syria; and behold, they are in Hazazontamar, which is Engedi."*
>
> *And Jehoshaphat feared, and set himself to seek the LORD, and proclaimed a fast throughout all Judah.*

And Judah gathered themselves together to ask help of the LORD; even out of all the cities of Judah they came to seek the LORD.....

Then upon Jahaziel the son of Zechariah, the son of Benaiah, the son of Jeiel, the son of Mattaniah, a Levite of the sons of Asaph, came the Spirit of the LORD in the midst of the congregation.

And he said, "Hearken ye, all Judah and ye inhabitants of Jerusalem, and thou King Jehoshaphat! Thus saith the LORD unto you: 'Be not afraid nor dismayed by reason of this great multitude; for the battle is not yours, but God's. Tomorrow go ye down against them. Behold, they come up by the cliff of Ziz, and ye shall find them at the end of the brook, before the Wilderness of Jeruel. Ye shall not need to fight in this battle. Set yourselves, stand ye still, and see the salvation of the LORD with you, O Judah and Jerusalem.' Fear not, nor be dismayed. Tomorrow go out against them, for the LORD will be with you."

And Jehoshaphat bowed his head with his face to the ground, and all Judah and the inhabitants of Jerusalem fell before the LORD, worshiping the LORD.

And the Levites, of the children of the Kohathites and of the children of the Korahites, stood up to praise the LORD God of Israel with a loud voice on high.

And they rose early in the morning and went forth into the Wilderness of Tekoa; and as they went forth, Jehoshaphat stood and said, "Hear me, O Judah, and ye inhabitants of Jerusalem: Believe in the LORD your

God; so shall ye be established. Believe His prophets; so shall ye prosper."

And when he had consulted with the people, he appointed singers unto the LORD who should praise the beauty of holiness as they went out before the army, and to say, "Praise the LORD, for His mercy endureth forever."

And when they began to sing and to praise, the LORD set ambushes against the children of Ammon, Moab, and Mount Seir, who had come against Judah; and they were smitten.

For the children of Ammon and Moab stood up against the inhabitants of Mount Seir utterly to slay and destroy them; and when they had made an end of the inhabitants of Seir, every one helped to destroy another.

And when Judah came toward the watchtower in the wilderness, they looked unto the multitude; and behold, they were dead bodies fallen to the earth, and none escaped.

And when Jehoshaphat and his people came to take away the spoil from them, they found among them in abundance both riches with the dead bodies and precious jewels, which they stripped off for themselves, more than they could carry away; and they were three days in gathering the spoil, it was so much. —2 Chronicles 20:1-4, 14-25

When you look at this story, when they fasted and prayed, God gave them answer through His prophet and directed them on what to do to have victory. But looking at the situation naturally, there was no change. It was left for them to trust God and His Word or continue to look at the situation and mourn like many of us does in these days. Their praise was a sign of their trust in God and what He said. Figuratively, they were telling the situation "Our God is bigger than you". The Bible says in 2 Chronicles 20:22 that the moment they started to praise God, God set an ambush against their enemy. Our Praises move God to leave the throne to manifest what He has promised and that is a confirmation of Psalm 22:3.

> *But Thou art holy, O Thou that inhabitest the praises of Israel.* —Psalm 22:3

When God came into the situation, within 24 hours the situation that looked impossible became possible and more than enough that it took them three days to gather their harvest. That is the power of praise.

In Acts 16:25-26, we see the same situation with Paul and Silas; they prayed and sang, God was moved again and chains were broken and closed doors were opened.

> *And at midnight Paul and Silas prayed and sang praises unto God, and the prisoners heard them. And suddenly there was a great earthquake, so that the foundations of the prison were shaken; and immediately all the doors were opened and everyone's bands were loosed.* —Acts 16:25-26

I don't know the chains around you right now as you read this book, but no matter the chain, set up an altar of praise and invite the God that answers with fire to hammer into that situation. He is a God who does wonders in praises. Let your praise go high and watch God take the battle from your hand and cause you to celebrate instead of mourning.

Who is like unto Thee, O LORD, among the gods? Who is like Thee, glorious in holiness, fearful in praises, doing wonders. —Exodus 15:11

The devil understands the power of praise, and that is why he constantly sends the enemies of praise against believers to hinder our victory over him. Some of these enemies of praise are as follows:

1. Murmuring and complaining. Everything you murmur about in life never grows but diminishes. Murmuring displeases God and opens the door for the destroyer. As a child of God, any time you complain, you invite defeat into your life. The Israelites murmured after God had given them the assurance of taking them into the promise land, but their murmuring kept them away from their promised land (1 Corinthians 10:10-11, Numbers 11:1).

2. Another enemy of praise is sorrow. Praise from an unhappy heart is a noise in the ears of God. We are admonished in Colossians 3:16 on how to sing to Him from our heart. And one of the sources of sorrow is hopelessness; but remember that as far as you are connected to the Lord, there is no situation in your life that is hopeless (Ecclesiastes 9:4, Jeremiah 29:11, Isaiah 51:11, Proverbs 4:18).

   How do you make yourself joyful in a rough situation? Remember that if the Lord can save you and washed you in the blood of His Son Jesus Christ, when you did not know Him, He is able to see you through in that situation right now; therefore, chose to bless His name through praise (Psalm 103:1-3).

3. Another enemy of praise is another 'god.' Jesus called money another god. If money is your source of happiness, you can never praise God sincerely. Why? Money comes and goes, and you can only be happy when it comes and when you cannot lay your

hands on it, everybody, including your loved ones, becomes your problem, plus God. This will hinder your praise. Let the Lord be your God both in good and in bad times. If He is your source of joy, whether there is money or not, you will still praise Him because the joy of the Lord is your strength (1 Timothy 6:10-11).

4. Offense. Offense is a negative reaction from an unpleasant condition. Offense hinders praise; it brings internal battle in your life and causes serious diseases (cancer, arthritis, mental problems, etc.). Don't be offended towards God when your breakthrough is not yet in your hands, but have patience and praise Him. John the Baptist was beheaded because of offense, but Paul and Silas were in the same position but were delivered because they praised Him (Matthew 11:3-6, Matthew 18:7, Acts 16:25-26).

5. Covetousness. Covetous people are never satisfied, so they run from one place to another looking for things that are not really necessary. But because others have them, they want them, too, and if they fail to get them, they are broken. (Luke 12:15, 1 Timothy 6:6-7).

Praise has also some benefits. Let us see the benefits of praise:

1. Praise provokes harvest. Praise causes fruitfulness in the kingdom of God. Behind every prosperous life is a mysterious praise. Praise releases heavenly rain into our lives. When you praise God in tough situations, He causes rain to fall upon you and when rain falls upon you, everything that was dying in your life will start to blossom (Psalm 67:5-6, Joel 2:23-27).

2. Praise releases His power on your behalf for divine intervention. When Paul and Silas were on their life mission, the enemy tried to stop them but Paul was wise enough to employ the weapon of praise. As they praised God, divine power was released and delivered them from the chains of the enemy and they went forth and accomplished their mission (Isaiah 30:29-31, Acts 16:25-26).

3. Praise releases fresh anointing (the power of God) upon our lives, which results in the breaking of yokes. It forces your enemies to give up on you. When a man or woman is anointed, the powers of darkness become ineffective against his or her life. You are equipped with power to make wealth. That power is ability and wisdom, which are principal things. Anointing also causes favor to follow you. The height anybody will attain in the Kingdom of God depends on the grace of God upon him or her. Grace is unmerited favor (Psalm 92:1-4, 10-11, Isaiah 10:27, Deuteronomy 8:18, Psalm 66:3, Psalm 5:12, Daniel 1:9).

4. Praise guarantees your protection: A praiseful person is always in His presence; that is why David was able to escape death several times when Saul attempted to kill him(Psalm 91:1-8, Psalm 23:4).

5. Praise beautifies you, mostly when it is in dance. Praiseful people remain young all the days of their lives. When you give God what He loves, He gives you what you want (He will beautify every ugly area in your life and crown you with a garment of praise, which is joy). You need joy to succeed in life (Psalm 149:1-5, Nehemiah 8:10, and Isaiah 61:3).

6. Praise causes supernatural uplifting. It does not matter how low people may think you are right now. God is the one that lifts up and brings down men and women. Jabez was despised by his family, but when Jabez recognized that his destiny was not in the hands of men but in the hands of God, he went and called upon the Lord and the Word of God said that God granted him his request. Today all generations read of the prosperous Jabez but nobody hears of Jabez's brothers or sisters. Your praise in your lowly state now will cause you to walk among princes and princesses tomorrow (Psalm 113:1-4, 7-9, 1 Chronicles 4:9-10, Habakkuk 3:17-19).

PATIENCE

After you have prayed, engage this tool of patience and praise. The more time you spend in His presence praising and thanking Him, the more He conforms your character to persevere for the victory ahead. No one succeeds in life without a good character, and that is what the presence of God does for us.

> *That ye be not slothful, but followers of them who through faith and patience inherit the promises.* — Hebrew 6:12

> *He staggered not at the promise of God through unbelief; but was strong in faith, giving glory to God. And being fully persuaded that, what he had promised, he was able also to perform.* —Romans 4:20-21

A patient man is never in a hurry. Abraham was fully persuaded that God is, and that He is able to perform what He promised. So whatever happened between the time of prayer and manifestation was not Abraham's concerned. All he knew was that God will do what He said; therefore, he gave him praise patiently waiting to see his "Isaac." Impatience has cost many their victory in prayer. Every successful man both in the kingdom of God and in the world today will testify that the road to victory is not smooth and the only one formula that will keep you focused is patience.

What is patience? It is calm endurance of pain or any provocation; forbearance; quiet and self-possessed waiting for something.

The Word of God said in Romans 4 that Abraham gave glory in this time of waiting. Why did he do that? The opposite of thanks is complains or murmuring because of pains or disappointment. So Abraham made up his mind that instead of aborting his harvest by complaining, he better praise God because praise will keep the enemy of harvest away from him and invite God into whatever circumstances that the enemy throws against him in order to stop the manifestation of his "Isaac."

I found out that the bigger your miracle or breakthrough, the more God works on our character in order to be able to be a blessing to others when our miracles manifest. So the delay for manifestation in some cases is not really bad but rather it is a season God "builds" us up character-wise so that we can manage the blessing well when it comes. Take Joseph's life as an example. The dream he saw took 13 years before manifestation; but within this period, Joseph was tested and he passed all the tests by patiently waiting for his enthronement.

I see your enthronement coming quickly, so don't give up, but build the altar of praise now and start to thank God for the past victory He gave to you and for the future one that is on the way.

Looking back at all I have shared in this book with the testimonies, I have no doubt that you will be listed among those that testify of His goodness in this season. It is your time—arise and shine, for the glory of the Lord has risen upon you. Shalom.

Apostle Dr. Victor Mebele is the Senior Pastor of
Global House of Prayer, Curacao
West Indies
Contact: ghpcuracao@hotmail.com

He is also the authors of the following books:

1. *The Secret of Answered Prayers*
2. *Locate Your Adversary*
3. *Let Go*
4. *Silent No More*
5. *Show Me Your Friend (I Will Tell You Who You Are)*
6. *Living Successfully*
7. *We Can, Yes We Can*
8. *You Are Created To Rule & Reign*

Printed in the United States
By Bookmasters